How to Become a

Dynamic
Speaker

Power to Move the Heart!

Rose Weiner

WeinerMedia.com

maranatha publications

A Maranatha Book
2013

Cover Design: Rose Weiner - Incorporates Painting of *Patrick Henry's Celebrated Speech Against the Stamp Act before the House of Burgesses, Virginia* by *Peter F. Rothermel.*

For Study Books and Daily Inspiration
Visit Our Website:

weinermedia.com

For more information write or call:
WeinerMedia@gmail.com

Maranatha Publications
P.O. Box 1799
Gainesville, Florida 32614
(352) 375-6000

PUBLISHER CATALOGING-IN-PUBLICATION DATA

Weiner, Rose, 1948

Learn how to inspire audiences. Helpful illustrations and practical advice from history, the Bible, and modern life. Analyze the text of America's best speakers. Learn how the spoken word has changed the world. Over 20 internet links to great speeches. Inspirational.

ISBN: 978-0-938558-19-4

1. Public Speaking I.Title

PN4192.C55

808.51   2032909547

Table of Contents

Why Everyone Should Know
How to Become a
Dynamic Speaker

One of the remarkable things about the early church is they were irresistible communicators. People found it hard to resist the wisdom with which they spoke. They were anointed with boldness - with the Holy Spirit and power - and they were great preachers. "But how can they call on Him to save them unless they believe in Him?" asks Paul. "And how can they believe in Him if they have never heard about Him? And how can they hear about Him unless someone tells them? So faith comes from hearing, that is by hearing the Word of God." (Rom. 10:14-15,17)

The Gospel must be spoken to others so they can hear and believe. Jesus promised all of His followers that an anointing would be given to them to speak messages from God. Jesus taught His disciples, "What you hear whispered in the ear, shout it from the housetops." And He promised, "For it is not you who will be speaking—it will be the Spirit of your Father speaking through you." (Matt. 10:20) Among His last words to His followers were these: "Go into all the world and preach the Good News to everyone, make disciples of all nations, teach them to observe everything I have taught you." Then He gave this promise, "I will be with you always even to the end of the world."

Besides being able to tell the Gospel, we all need to be able to communicate effectively about everything in life, whether it is in a one-on-one conversation, in a small group setting, or before large audiences. We need to be able to tell our testimony of what God has done for us; we need to be able to communicate our point of view and get our ideas across. We need to be able to speak effectively so we can persuade others, address the media, give interviews, make sales, communicate at work, converse with our clients, make progress in school, grow in human relationships, be successful statesmen or stateswomen, and be understood in our personal relationships, in our family, or in whatever circumstances we may encounter in our daily lives. As Christians, especially, we should be good - no, great - communicators.

This book was written to help people achieve these ends. In its short form, a portion of this book first appeared years ago as an article for a monthly periodical.   It has been used by many who have wanted to get a handle on how to speak more effectively, regardless of the venue.   It has even been used as required reading for a college course on speaking. Over the years, I have come across many inspirational thoughts as well as some simple yet profound things the Lord has shown me about speaking. I have always wanted to add them to this text, but either for lack of time or a lack of diligence, I just never got around to it.

Recently, I sat down to expand this book and to recall the things the Lord has shown me. Almost immediately the thoughts and ideas that I wanted to write down came flooding back into my mind, sometimes almost faster than I could write them down. True to what Jesus promised, "The Helper, the Holy Spirit, whom the Father will send in My name, He will teach you all things, and bring to your remembrance all things that I said to you." (John 14:26)

The Idea of Receiving

What does it take to be a really great speaker? Good speaking most often is just like good writing - it is not about straining, trying to think something up - it is more about listening and receiving something from a Source greater than yourself, and then writing down or speaking what you are hearing. It is knowing God as your ongoing, unlimited supply. David, the great psalmist, spoke of his encounter with the Voice of God's Eternal Spirit: "The heavens declare the glory of God; And the firmament shows His handiwork. Day unto day utters speech, and night unto night reveals knowledge. There is no speech nor language where their voice is not heard. Their line has gone out through all the earth, and their words to the end of the world." (Psalm 19)

Jesus explained it this way: "Whatever I tell you in the dark, speak in the light; and what you hear in the ear, preach on the housetops. You are the light of the world. A city that is set on a hill cannot be hidden. Nor do they light a lamp and put it under a basket, but on a lamp-stand, and it gives light to all in the house. Let your light so shine before men, that they may see your good works and glorify your Father in heaven." (Matt. 5:14-16)

Emerson describes the phenomena of receiving from God's Eternal Voice in his essay, *The Poet:* "For poetry was all written before time was, and whenever we are so finely organized that we can penetrate into that region where the air is music, we hear those primal warblings, and attempt to write them down . . . those of more delicate ear write down these cadences more faithfully, and these transcripts, though imperfect, become the songs of the nations."

It is often our desire to appear smart, our wish to be thought of as a fabulous speaker, our desire to glorify ourselves, or our fear of what someone might think about us that can block the energy flow of God's Spirit. All this is just another name for pride, which can cause us a great deal of problems. "Pride goes before the fall, and a haughty spirit before stumbling,"[1] the ancient Hebrew King reminds us. Whether we want to look great, or fear we are going to look bad, both attitudes are still pride - the second appears to be humble, but it is only in appearance, not in reality. Fear of failure and pride of accomplishment are just opposite ends of the same stick.

Dante, in *Purgatorio*, tells us about the place of the proud in the Eternal hereafter which he called "The First Terrace of the Mountain of Purgatory." Here the proud are doomed to go around the "Mountain" on a narrow path with a big burden on their back. The burden is their ego - their desire for excellence - their desire to be recognized by others for doing things with perfection. Around the Mountain they must walk until they are willing to let the burden go. Dante tells us that on the First Terrace, the Mountain is made of white marble with many beautiful life-like sculptures carved on its side, which give examples of humility.

One sculpture is of Mary the mother of Jesus "to whom came the gracious verdict that reversed our woe, when the long-wept-for peace, by Heaven's decree, to men was granted." Before the archangel she bows low with the Latin inscription *Ecce Ancilla Dei*, that is to say, "Behold, the maidservant of God." Another carving is of David, "the Psalmist, more and less than king," who is portrayed dancing before the Ark of God as he brought it up to Jerusalem "with garments girded high," while Michal, his wife, from a palace window, looks on him with scorn. [2]

The Motley Crew

Under the feet of the proud, sculptured in the pavement, are "carvings as marvelous as those on the cliff face" of various figures who fell through the sin of pride. The penitent are bound to see these figures because of the burden on their backs that forces them to keep their faces toward the ground. Their goal in their journey is to identify the sins of those depicted here in their own heart, repent of them, and put those sins under their feet.

In the pavement there is a carving of "Lucifer, heaven's noblest, raised by pride and cast from heaven like lightning." There is Nimrod depicted "with the nations raging around him." Under Nimrod's direction the Tower of Babel was built in the plain of Shinar. Josephus, the Jewish historian of the first century, writes that the Jews understood that Nimrod encouraged people in the sin of pride and persuaded them not to believe that God was responsible for their happiness, "but to believe that it was their own courage which procured that happiness." Josephus writes, "Nimrod also gradually changed the government into tyranny, seeing no other way of turning men from the fear of God, but to bring them into a constant dependence on his power."

The Hebrew Sages tell that Nimrod taught the people to trust in themselves and to secure their future by building a tower high enough to reach heaven so that the flood waters would never be able to destroy them. Because the people refused to go out and repopulate the earth as God had commanded and trust in God's promise of protection, God confused their language and scattered them throughout the world. They formed nations which ultimately became antagonistic toward each other.

Engraved in the pavement is also a sculpture of Rehoboam fleeing for his life in his chariot, being pursued by his enemy. When he became King after his father Solomon died, the men of Israel asked him to lighten their tax burden. He rejected the counsel of the older men of the kingdom, who advised him to listen to the voice of the people, and instead took the advice of the proud young men. In pride, he said, "Yes, my father laid heavy burdens on you, but I'm going to make them even heavier! My father beat you with whips, but I will beat you with scorpions!" As a result, the majority of Israel refused his kingship, and Israel was divided into two separate kingdoms - the Kingdom of Israel and the Kingdom of Judah.

Another scene engraved in the pavement depicts the downfall of Sennacherib who was King of Assyria and responsible for the Kingdom of Israel becoming the "Lost Tribes." He was sent by God to take the Kingdom of Israel into captivity because they had turned to idols. Nation after nation had fallen before him, and he had smashed and burned their idols and mocked their gods.

Flushed with pride from all of his victories, Sennacherib thought too highly of himself. He came up to Hezekiah, King of the Kingdom of Judah, and demanded his surrender as well. He sent this message to the people: "Do not let Hezekiah mislead you when he says, 'The Lord will deliver us.' Have the gods of any nations ever delivered their lands from the hand of the King of Assyria? Where are the gods of Hamath and Arpad? Have they rescued Samaria (the Kingdom of Israel) from my hand? Who of all the gods of these countries has been able to save their lands from me? How then can the Lord deliver Jerusalem from my hand?"

King Hezekiah spread the letter Sennacherib had sent before the Lord and asked God to deliver Judah. God listened and sent this word to Sennacherib written by the prophet Isaiah:

> "Against whom have you raised your voice and lifted your eyes in pride? Against the Holy One of Israel! By your messengers you have ridiculed the Lord. You will not enter

this city or shoot an arrow here. I will defend this city and save it."

Then Isaiah tells us:

Then the angel of the Lord went out and put to death a hundred and eighty-five thousand in the Assyrian camp. When the people got up the next morning—there were all the dead bodies! So Sennacherib, King of Assyria, broke camp and withdrew. He returned to Nineveh and stayed there. One day, while he was worshiping in the temple of his god Nisrok, his sons Adrammelek and Sharezer killed him with the sword, and they escaped to the land of Ararat. (portions of Isa. 36)

Why did Sennacherib's sons kill him? Because of lost honor and pride. Their father chose his youngest son whose mother was his concubine to be heir to the throne instead of one of them. They were the eldest and sons of the Queen. Sennacherib's portrait reminds us of Israel's disobedience which caused them to be scattered among the nations and of God's judgment on the wicked, who think they will not have to answer to God. The scene is of him sprawled dead on the pavement as his murderous sons withdraw as he reaps the fruit of his pride.

Another carving is of King Saul, depicted as pierced and dead by his own weapon. He, too, disobeyed God and was brought down by pride. When God rejected him from being King, he showed no concern about it, except to plead with the prophet Samuel saying, "Please come and honor me before the people."[3]

In contrast, neither Mary the mother of Jesus nor David, who are both examples of true humility, cared what people thought about them - they surrendered themselves to God's purposes. On the other hand, Satan and the rest of his crew were motivated by their desire to be great and to be admired. They turned others from being God's servants to try to make them their own. They were lifted up in pride, which ultimately brought their downfall.

Playing to the Audience of One

Once a master violinist was given a standing ovation after his performance. No matter how much the audience applauded, he refused to take a bow. Finally with head bowed low, he left the stage. Asked about it later he said, "My teacher was sitting in the balcony. I was waiting for him to stand in approval, for if I don't have his approval, all the applause of the crowd is meaningless."

As we depend on the Great Creator who makes His dwelling within us, we will be free from being dependent on the approval or disapproval of others. As A.W. Tozer points out, "This is how the martyrs could stand alone against the universal disapproval of all mankind and say, 'my heart is full of gardens and fountains.' "[4] Like the master violinist, we will play to the audience of "One."

To this very thing, Jesus himself calls us: "If you try to save your life, you will lose it, but if you lose your life for My sake you will find it. Whoever wants to follow after Me must deny himself, take up his cross and follow Me, or he cannot be My disciple. What does it profit a man if he gains the world but loses his own soul? For whoever is ashamed of Me and My words in this adulterous and sinful generation, the Son of Man will also be ashamed of him when He comes in the glory of His Father with the holy angels." (Mark 8:34-38)

What we need now more than ever is uncompromised, fearless oratory - inspired messages from the realms of the Eternal Spirit that will call us to change the way we live. We need heaven-breathed messages to inspire our children and nations to stand in awe of God, and through His mighty power accomplish great things for God's kingdom, both on earth and in heaven and for the blessing of the human race - in the way God measures greatness.

As you will discover, the moment you realize that you are taking God as your Partner and as the Source of your inspiration will be the moment when you will find that whatever you need for the project you are attempting will be handed to you. When you accept God as your Helper, you will find that there is a Second Voice within, a Higher Harmonic, leading you onward and upward, and you will find help everywhere.

The purpose of this little book, then, is not just to learn effective methods of communication - it is to show how to receive and communicate great ideas and thoughts with others in such a way that it will bring life-changing results and bring prosperity and blessing to whoever is willing to hear. Paul exhorted the early church, "Always be prepared to give an account of the hope that is within you." He reminds us that it is through "the foolishness of preaching" that the lost find eternal life.

That is why the Scriptures say, "How beautiful are the feet of messengers who bring good news! Who proclaim peace. Who bring glad tidings of good things, who say unto Zion your God reigns!" It is God's reign that we are all called to proclaim - and His kingdom's reign speaks to all areas of life and living. (Isa. 52:7)

One

On Fire with a Message!

As Christians, we are called to be the greatest communicators on earth. And why shouldn't we be? We have the greatest message to communicate to the world. Our words hold weight and power when they are based in Truth and are inspired and anointed by God's Holy Spirit. Down through the ages, Christianity has been known historically as "The Great Confession." Although the word "confession" is usually thought of in negative terms, such as acknowledging sin or wrongdoing, "confession" in the positive sense means to publicly declare a belief in something and stick to that belief, regardless of opposition or personal cost.

At the time of the founding of the United States, this was what our Founders understood as the meaning of the word *confessor.* In *Webster's 1828 Dictionary of the American Language,* the first American Dictionary ever written, Noah Webster, one of our Founding Fathers, defined *confessor* as "one who makes a profession of his faith in the Christian religion. The word is appropriately used to denote one who avows his religion in the face of danger, and adheres to it in defiance of persecution and torture. It was formerly used as synonymous with the word *martyr.*"

History and the Bible are full of resplendent examples of those whose unforgettable words and fiery speeches have changed the course of nations and the destinies of peoples. Who doesn't stand amazed at the boldness of Peter's confession on the day of Pentecost: "So let everyone in Israel know for certain that God has made this Jesus, whom you crucified, to be both Lord and Messiah!" Luke, the author of the book of Acts, tells us that Peter's words were so powerful they "pierced the hearts" of those who were listening - so much so that they cried out, "What shall we do?" And as a result, 3,000 people repented and were baptized in one day and the church began.

John Huss, Priest and Martyr

Consider the powerful words of John Huss in 1415 AD, a priest from Czechoslovakia. Because Huss refused the demand of an apostate Church to deny the Truth that he had been preaching from the Bible, he was led away to be burned at the stake. At a public trial in the Council of Constance in Germany, Bishops and the Emperor asked Huss to retract the things that he had been preaching from the Bible that contradicted the traditions of the Roman Church.

Here is the bold account of the *Confession of John Huss* recorded by nineteenth-century historian Charles Coffin in *The Story of Liberty*:

Jan Huss at the Council of Constance *by Václav Brožík*

The Archbishop reads one of the charges, "He has taught that a priest polluted with deadly sins cannot administer the sacrament of the altar, which is heretical."

"I still say that every act of a priest ladened with deadly sins is an abomination in the sight of God," Huss answers.

Ah! That is a home-thrust. Bishops, archbishops, cardinals and priests who are living with women to whom they have not been married never will forgive this heretic for saying that.

Huss turns to the people and says, "The bishops want me to retract; but if I were to do so, I would be a liar before God."

"Silence, you stiff-necked heretic!" the archbishop replies.

They place a silver goblet of wine in his hand, and then take it away.

"O thou cursed Judas! We take from thee this chalice in which the blood of Christ is offered for the remission of thy sins."

There is no blanching in his cheeks. "Confiding in my God and Savior, I indulge the hope that He will not take from me the cup of salvation, and I trust that I shall drink of it this day in His kingdom," Huss replies.

Greater than Emperor, Pope or Archbishop is John Huss, standing there beneath the vaulted roof of the old hall. None so calm, so peaceful, so quiet of heart as he - soon to become one of Liberty's great sons. None so shamefaced, so insignificant, as Sigismund, Emperor of Germany. One word from his lips would set the prisoner free; but his craven heart has yielded to the demand of those who are thirsting for the blood of Huss. Although the Emperor promised Huss safe conduct if he would come and defend his teaching, they have made him believe that he is not obliged to keep faith with a heretic. Yet, he knows that he is committing an act which, ever as he recalls it, will redden his cheeks with shame.

"Let him be accursed of God and man eternally," the archbishop pronounces.

In all the assembly of prelates there is not one kindly face or look of pity.

"I am willing thus to suffer for the Truth in the name of Christ."

They place a paper cap upon his head - a mock crown - with figures of the devil upon it and this inscription: *This is a Heretic.*

The procession moves out into the street through a bonfire of Huss' books. He smiles when he sees the parchments curling in the air. They can burn the books, but Truth and Liberty will live forever.

"He goes as though he is on his way to a banquet," Bishop Silvius says.

"What is that Huss is saying?"

"I will extol Thee, O Lord, for You have lifted me up and have not made my foes to rejoice over me."

Huss turns to the people and says, "Do not believe that I have taught anything but the Truth."

He is going to testify for the Truth, why should he fear? Truth and Liberty are eternal. Sticks are piled around him. The executioner stands with the torch.

"Renounce your error," shouts the Duke of Bavaria.

"I have taught no error. The truths I have taught I will seal with my blood."

"Burn him!"

The executioner lights the fire. What is it the people hear coming from the sheet of flame? "Glory be to God on high and on earth peace good will toward men. We praise You, we bless You, we worship You, we glorify You, we give *thanks* to You for Your great glory."

As the smoke circles his head, Huss utters his last words, "Thou who takes away the sins of the world have mercy on me."[5]

Although the religious leaders of the day were able to kill the body of John Huss, the message of Truth that he brought kept speaking down through the years. Huss had preached the Truth. He had preached against the immorality of the clergy, the worship of relics, and buying pardons for the forgiveness of sin.

On the walls of the Chapel of Bethlehem where he was the priest, Huss had posted pictures to contrast his meaning. He hung a painting of Jesus riding into Jerusalem on a donkey, and opposite it, a painting of the Pope with his triple crown riding in his accustomed fashion of sitting on a throne, being carried on the shoulders of priests, with trumpets blaring to announce his entrance. Adjacent to this, Huss hung a picture of Jesus kneeling down washing the disciples' feet. Next to it was the Pope seated on his papal throne with people kneeling down kissing his feet. Huss had preached that Christ, not the Pope, was the Head of the Church. He preached that Church leaders should be examples of God-fearing integrity.

John Huss, the Results of His Preaching

The multitude of people who followed Huss continued to believe just as Huss had taught them. Under the leadership of Count Zinzendorf, the Hussites became known as the Moravians. They started a prayer chain that lasted one hundred years and sent out 2,500 missionaries all over the world. Their prayers helped birth the Protestant Reformation in the sixteenth century. The Moravians were instrumental in the conversion of John Wesley in the seventeenth century, who became the founder of Methodism. Wesley was the leader of the Great Awakening that swept England. On the shores of North America, his missionaries would fan the flames of Spiritual Awakening in the young British colonies. That was the Awakening that gave rise to American Independence. [6]

Over the next 5 centuries the leaders of the Catholic Church felt justified in their actions. However, on December 18, 1999, 548 years after the execution of John Huss, Pope John Paul II visited Prague, Czechoslovakia, and on behalf of the Catholic Church expressed "deep regret for the cruel death inflicted on Huss."[7]

Watch this inspiring movie about John Huss and listen to his famous speech - tremendous delivery: John Huss, the Story of a Martyr: https://goo.gl/VkSBY9

Europe - 100 Years after the Death of Huss

For 100 years after the death of Huss, in the rest of Catholic Europe, the Bible continued its testimony in sackcloth and ashes, confined to the shelves of dusty monasteries, waiting for the next preacher of righteousness. Among Huss' last words as he was burning at the stake was this prophecy, "In one hundred years, God will raise up a man whose calls for reform will not be suppressed."[8] The year was 1415 A.D.

In 1515, one hundred years later, Martin Luther was made the official representative of Saxony for the Roman Church. One day while Luther was rummaging through books in the monastery library, he discovered a volume of sermons by John Huss. Evidently, this was one of Huss' books that had "miraculously" escaped the bonfires. If God wants a book preserved he has many ways to do it now how many fires are kindled to destroy it. Luther later wrote, "I was overwhelmed with astonishment. I could not understand for what cause they had burnt so great a man, who explained the Scriptures with so much gravity and skill." [9]

Luther also was studying the Bible he had found in the monastery library and was preaching its truth at the University of Wittenberg where he was a professor. Books were rare and very few people owned a Bible. Besides this, the Bible was written in Latin and very few people could read Latin or read at all for that matter. As Luther studied the Bible, he began to see the teachings of the Roman Church in that day were totally contradicted by the Truth in the Scriptures. Like Huss before him, he issued a call for reforms in Catholic doctrine to bring the teachings of the Church in line with Scripture.

In 1517, Luther nailed his *95 Theses of Contention* to the door of Wittenberg Chapel to call the Roman Church to reform the very same abuses that Huss preached against. Luther took up the hammer for Truth, it would be as if thousands of Husses had risen from the dead. What does this tell us? Nothing can stop the Truth from having its way! No martyr's fire or opposition of man can extinguish its flame.

William Cullen Bryant, 19th-century American poet, said it this way:

> Truth, crushed to earth, shall
> rise again;
> The eternal years of God are
> hers;
> But Error, wounded, writhes in pain,
> And dies among his worshippers.

God watches over His Word to perform it. It will strike the mark and accomplish everything the Lord sent it to do. "Is not My word like a fire?" says the Lord, "And like a hammer that shatters the rock." (Jer. 23:29)

Martin Luther, Father of the Protestant Reformation

Consider the immortal words of Martin Luther, Reformer and Father of the Protestant Reformation. Luther was called to appear before the Bishops and the Emperor of Germany at the Diet of Worms in 1521 to give an account of his teaching.. He

Luther Before the Diet of Worms by Anton von Werner

preached against indulgences, which was buying pardons for the forgiveness of sin. He taught that the just should live by faith, not by trying to earn their salvation or paying money. They were to trust in the shed blood of Jesus alone for the forgiveness of sin. Pope Leo X asked Luther to renounce his teachings. If not Luther would be excommunicated from the Catholic Church.

To be excommunicated meant that Luther would be turned over to the devil by the Pope and condemned for eternity to the flames of hell. Luther refused. Pope Leo issued a final ban on Martin Luther's books and offered to give Luther one last chance to repent for writing them before he excommunicated him from the Church and committed him to the flames of hell forever. To make his recantation public, Leo had commanded Luther to appear before the council at the Diet of Worms to denounce his writings. Luther's friends had urged him not to go, reminding him of John Huss' fate one hundred years earlier. Luther would not be turned aside. "I shall go to Worms though there be as many devils as tiles on the rooftops."

Here is the account of Luther's testimony before the Diet of Worms as retold by Charles Coffin in *The Story of Liberty*:

> Noblemen escort Dr. Luther to the city. The Emperor did not think that he would come. The Pope's ambassadors are disappointed. They did not want Doctor Luther to come. They hoped he would be frightened and stay away and not obey the order, and then the emperor would be obliged to seize him.
>
> "Here he is. What shall we do?" the Emperor asks.
>
> "The council must be held," he decides.
>
> The bell strikes four - the hour when Doctor Luther must appear before the council.
>
> The Emperor is seated on a throne. Around him are Spanish knights in gleaming armor, his brother, the Archduke Ferdinand, and six Princes. There are eighty dukes, thirty archbishops and bishops, seven ambassadors of France and England, and the Pope's ambassador - more than two hundred great dignitaries in all.
>
> No wonder the Pope did not want the council to meet. Has he not forbidden Doctor Luther's speaking? Yet, here he is about to address the greatest assembly ever seen in Germany! Has not the Pope forbidden everybody from listening to him? Yet here is an immense multitude waiting to hear what he will say. Has not the Pope declared that he is an outlaw, with no rights that any one is bound to respect? Yet, here he is recognized as having rights which the Emperor is bound to acknowledge. [10]

"I have two questions to ask you," says the Archbishop of Trier, opening the examination and pointing to some books on the table. "Did you write these books?"

"I do not deny having written those books," is his answer after the titles are read.

"Will you take back what you have written?"

Having been informed that he answers in the peril of his life, Luther responded, "As to taking back anything in accordance with the Word of God, I must act deliberately. I will give you my answer tomorrow."

The council breaks up for the day. The crowd in the streets admire the courage of a man who dares to stand by his rights and for the Truth in such an assembly - who even compels all the archbishops and the emperor to wait upon him. 11

On the following day, the examination reconvenes. The Emperor and the assembled Princes and Nobles of the Empire are in attendance. In the presence of that powerful and titled assembly, the lowly born Reformer seemed awed and awkward. Noting his struggle, several of the German Princes approach him, and one of them whispers: "Fear not them which kill the body, but are not able to kill the soul."

Another says: "When you are brought before governors and kings for My sake, it shall be given you, by the Spirit of your Father, what you shall say."

They are quoting the Bible. In this hour of testing, Luther is encouraged by the Word of God from some of the world's great Princes. Dr. Luther stands in the council. He is about to speak. The Archbishop of Trier cannot bear to have a man whom the Pope has forbidden to speak stand there and compel everybody to listen to him.

"Will you, or will you not retract?" shouts the Archbishop.

Dr. Luther looks around. He is in the council's hands. What shall he say? Shall he take all back? God has walked by his side; shall he distrust the One who has protected him this far?

"Dr. Luther, are you willing to recant the errors contained in your books?" Eck, the interrogator, questions.

"I am a mere man, and not God, yet I will defend myself after the example of Jesus Christ, who said: 'If I have spoken evil, bear witness against me.' How much more should I, who am but dust and ashes and so prone to error, desire that every one should bring forward what he can against my doctrine.

"Therefore, most serene Emperor, and you illustrious Princes, and all, whether high or low, who hear me, I implore you by the mercies of God to prove to me by the writings of the prophets and apostles that I am in error. As soon as I shall be convinced, I will instantly retract all my errors, and will myself be the first to seize my writings, and commit them to the flames.

"What I have just said I think will clearly show that I have well considered and weighed the dangers to which I am exposing myself; but far from being dismayed by them, I rejoice exceedingly to see the Gospel this day, as of old, a cause of disturbance and disagreement. It is the character and destiny of God's Word. 'I came not to send peace unto the earth, but a sword,' said Jesus Christ."

The interrogator is Dr. Eck, an official in the administration of the Archbishop of Trier. Luther has not composed his remarks for reading from a manuscript, but continues to speak impromptu:

"God is wonderful and awful in His counsels. Let us have a care, lest in our endeavors to arrest discords, we be bound to fight against the holy Word of God and bring down upon our heads a frightful deluge of inextricable dangers, present disaster, and everlasting desolations .... Let us have a care lest the reign of the young and noble Prince, the Emperor Charles, on whom next to God we build so many hopes, should not only commence but continue, lest we terminate its course under the most fatal auspices.

"I might cite examples drawn from the oracles of God. I might speak of Pharaohs, of Kings of Babylon, or of Israel, who were never more contributing to their own ruin than when, by measures in appearances most prudent, they thought to establish their authority! 'God removes the mountains and they know not.'"

Having spoken in German, Luther is asked to repeat the whole speech (of which this excerpt is a small part) again in Latin because the young Emperor Charles is not fond of German. Although bathed with sweat, Luther gives his whole discourse again in "undiminished power."

At this Eck, his examiner, retorts, "You have not given any answer to the inquiry put to you. You are not to question the decisions of the councils—you are required to return a clear and distinct answer. Will you or will you not retract?"
Finally, Luther could take no more.

"Since your most serene majesty and your high mightiness require of me a simple, clear, and direct answer, I will give one, and it is this: I cannot submit my faith either to the Pope or to the Council, because it is as clear as noonday that they have fallen into error and even into glaring inconsistency with themselves. If, then, I am not convinced by proof from Holy Scripture, or by cogent reasons, if I am not satisfied by the very text I have cited, and if my judgment is not in this way brought into subjection to God's Word, I neither can, nor will, retract anything; for it cannot be right for a Christian to speak against his conscience. I stand here and can say no more. God help me. Amen."

Luther leaves the room, but is summoned again.

"Doctor Luther," Eck demands in a fervent manner, "did you actually mean to say that councils have erred?"

"They have erred many times, in particular the Council of Constance," Luther replies.

"Doctor Luther," Eck says emphatically, "if you do not retract, the Emperor and the States of the Empire will proceed to consider how to deal with an obstinate heretic!" Luther replies, "May God be my Helper, but I can retract nothing."

"Doctor Luther, the council wants to remind you that you have not spoken with that humility which befits your condition."

"I have no other answer to give than that which I have already given."

The Emperor then made a sign to end the matter.

Martin Luther's Trial and Speech before the Diet of Worms
delivered by Joseph Fiennes and Jonathan Firth:
https://goo.gl/nxQ4kd

Luther's Secret

The power of the religious legates of Rome, who always made the kings and nobles of Europe tremble at any contradiction of their teaching and direction, was defied by a humble monk. The Spirit of Christ had spoken through Luther - he was bold, unrelenting, and unafraid. What was the secret of Martin Luther's great boldness? In the following prayer that Luther told that he prayed the morning before he was to appear at the Diet of Worms, we find his secret:

> My God, stand by me, against all the world's wisdom and reason. Not mine but Yours is the cause. I would prefer to have peaceful days and to be out of this turmoil. But Yours, O Lord, is this cause; it is righteous and eternal. Stand by me, You True Eternal God! In no man do I trust. Stand by me, O God, in the name of Your dear Son Jesus Christ, who shall be my Defense and Shelter, yes, my Mighty Fortress, through the might and strength of your Holy Spirit. Amen.[12]

Luther's words had been free from pride. He had stood in the blaze of Truth and the Spirit of Christ had answered his prayer. Later, Luther would write a hymn that is now famous all over the Christian world - *A Mighty Fortress is Our God* - which came to be known as *The Battle Hymn of the Reformation*. Consider the lyrics:

> A Mighty Fortress is our God,
> A bulwark never failing;
> Our Helper, He amid the flood
> Of mortal ills prevailing.
> For still our ancient foe
> Does seek to work us woe;
> His craft and power are great,

And armed with cruel hate,
On earth is not His equal.

Did we in our own strength confide,
Our striving would be losing,
Were not the right Man on our side,
The Man of God's own choosing.
You ask who that may be?
Christ Jesus, it is He;
Lord Sabbath, His name,
From age to age the same,
And He must win the battle.

And though this world, with devils filled
Should threaten to undo us;
We will not fear, for God has willed
His Truth to triumph through us.
The Prince of Darkness grim,
We tremble not for him;
His rage we can endure,
For lo, his doom is sure;
One little Word shall fell him.

That Word above all earthly power
No thanks to them, abideth;
The Spirit and the gifts are ours,
Thru Him who with us sideth.
Let goods and kindred go,
This mortal life also
The body they may kill;
God's Truth abideth still;
His kingdom is forever.

Listen to A Mighty Fortress is Our God:
https://goo.gl/RLx5DM

Luther, the Results of His Oratory

What were the results of Luther's bold stand for Truth? Historian Charles Coffin reflects in *The Story of Liberty*:

> Little does Luther know that out of it will come a great division in the Church; that thrones will be tumbled into the dust; that kings will go down, empires be rent asunder, lands be desolated by war; that there will be massacres and horrible outrages against the lives and liberties of men.

> If he could lift the veil that hides the future, he would see the streets of Paris and the vine-clad valleys of Italy drenched in blood. He would see fires kindled all over England for the burning of men and women, and children.

> He would see men hurled headlong from precipices, roasted over slow fires, starving in dungeons subjected to every form of cruelty; but this would be the beginning of the emancipation of men, the advance of Justice, Truth, and Liberty - the beginning of a new era in human affairs."

> Little did Luther know that the Christian Liberty he extolled that day in Worms - the right to hold an individual opinion, the right to read the Bible and interpret it for oneself - would one day find its way across treacherous seas.

> He did not know that Liberty and Religious Freedom would soon make their home in the New World on the shores of North America and birth a nation where freedom to worship God according to the dictates of one's own conscience would be the heritage of all. Little did he know that the Christian Liberty he so boldly proclaimed would give birth to a new civilization and a new era for the rights of man. Such are the

results of the bold proclamation of Truth - it is living and powerful, sharper than a two-edged sword. The Truth lives on through the ages and continues to do its work.

In 1620, the Pilgrims landed at Plymouth on the rockbound coast of North America, seeking freedom to worship God - the product of Luther's Protestant Reformation.

The Landing of the Pilgrims
Plate: Drawn by Charles Lucey and engraved by T. Phillibrown, 1859

Historical Note: God used Martin Luther in a marvelous way to help the world break free from the spiritual darkness of ecclesiastical bondage into the priesthood of every believer. Luther restored the doctrine of salvation by faith in the shed blood of Jesus Christ alone for the forgiveness of sins and re-established the Bible as the measurement of all Truth rather than the doctrines of men.

At this time of medieval darkness in Europe, the truth of salvation as taught from the pages of Scripture was just dawning on the minds of men. With the invention of the printing press, the Bible was made available to the common man. However, 1,200 years of darkness - known in history as the Dark Ages - had taken their toll, and many of the barbaric ways of men had not yet been transformed by the Word of God.

Luther like most of faith's heroes was not without flaws. When Luther first began his Reformation, he had held out great hope that the Roman Church would be persuaded to make his suggested reforms. He also had great hope for the salvation of the Jewish people. Luther read in Romans 11 that one day all of Israel would be saved and worked tirelessly for their salvation, trying to win them by argument and persuasion to belief in Jesus as their Messiah and the Savior of the world.

Luther was met with continual resistance and obstinacy from the majority of the Jewish people to such a point that he began to believe that it was impossible for the Jews to be saved. He became anti-Semitic and threw his lot in with burning Jewish synagogues. He was still blinded in this area by darkness. While this was a tragedy and cannot be justified, we are all inheritors of the measure of truth Luther championed and the understanding of Christian Liberty that inevitably led to the founding of our nation.

Watch Martin Luther Documentary - very powerful:
Part 1: https://goo.gl/nP6jHv
Part 2: https://goo.gl/Qo3Jz8

Two

Great American Speakers
of the 18th Century

Patrick Henry - 1736-1799
by George B. Matthews

Perhaps there is no better way to learn how to become a dynamic speaker than to study the texts of some of the greatest speeches ever given. Nowhere do we find a better collection of great speeches than those of our nation's best orators. When a person is being trained to detect counterfeit money, he doesn't study counterfeit money - he studies real money. This makes the counterfeit much easier to spot. As we study great speeches, we learn what a good speech is and what it takes not only to write a good speech, but also what it takes to give a powerful delivery that will move the hearts of our audience.

Patrick Henry Throws Down the Gauntlet

Patrick Henry emerged as a leader in the American colonies through his oratorical remarks against the Stamp Act. The British Parliament passed a law to tax the colonists for every piece of paper they used or had in their house. Imagine a garrison of soldiers coming to your house and searching through it to make sure every piece of paper was marked with a stamp with the King's picture on it to show you paid the tax. The colonists were furious. The tax was to be used to quarter ten thousand British troops near the Allegheny Mountains to "protect" the American frontier. The colonists were growing more and more uneasy and suspicious about the presence of so many British troops in America, and since their "rights" were being disrespected, they wondered what this might mean. According to the British Bill of Rights, no Englishman could be taxed without the consent of their legislative representatives.

This "right" went back to the signing of Magna Carta in 1215 AD, when the British noblemen wrested power from King John because he had taxied them against their will. Because they refused to give up their cattle to the King's men who wanted to take them at their whim, John sent his men to kill their sons or throw them into prison. From that day, the Parliament was formed to make laws to which both King and people must submit. The Magna Carta did not allow the British King to levy taxes without the consent of the people's representatives. This law had been in place for English people for over 500 years. The colonists' representatives were in America. They had no representatives in the British Parliament, and Britain had not submitted the matter to the colonial legislators in America for approval.

Patrick Henry, for one, believed the British government had gone too far and was breaking the law. A Stamp Act Congress was convened in Virginia, and Patrick Henry, an outstanding young lawyer and farmer, was one of the delegates. The air bristled with excitement when Henry arrived because he had already gained a reputation for sharp debate. Henry did not disappoint the offended Virginia legislators. He stood up and threw down the gauntlet, challenging the authority of the King and the British Parliament. Henry proposed seven resolutions to set aside these taxes as illegal, criticizing the British Parliament for acting outside the law. A fiery debate ensued. Although there was no written transcript of Henry's speech that day, eyewitnesses reported the following:

> When it was Henry's turn to take the floor again, Henry turned his criticism to King George III. With fiery eyes and the passion of a well-seasoned orator Henry thundered, "Caesar had his Brutus, Charles the First his Cromwell, and George the Third — "
>
> As the delegates readily recognized Henry's reference to assassinated leaders, some of them were appalled and perhaps a little frightened. These delegates rose from their seats, interrupted his speech, and cried out, "Treason! Treason!"
>
> Henry paused briefly, and quietly looked at the men who had made the accusations until they fell back into silence. Then calmly he finished his sentence: "... may profit by their example. If this be treason, make the most of it." (Never underestimate the power of the "pause" in a speech to captivate the audience and gain their undivided attention.)

Although there are no written drafts of Henry's speech, the oral history of its content and description of this moment was well-believed enough among those living at that time to prompt Peter Rothermel to paint the scene. Take a look for a moment at this painting called "Speech Against the Stamp Act" which appears on the front cover of this book. The artist depicts the fury that Henry's speech stirred up in those loyal to the King. Some men are pondering the speech thoughtfully. A few women in the balcony are huddled together in shock. One lady hangs over the balcony in suspense. Just under the word "Speaker" notice the man with the drawn sword. On the right we see George Washington, a member of the House of Burgesses, listening intently as a man whispers in his ear. In the balcony, a man puts forth his hand in resistance. At the bottom left, a man in a blue velvet jacket also extends his hand in resistance.

Notice the glove with an extended cuff, known as a *gauntlet*, on the floor in the painting. The practice of throwing a glove down on the ground when issuing a challenge is called "throwing down the gauntlet." The practice comes from the medieval ages. A gauntlet-wearing knight would challenge a fellow knight or enemy to a duel by throwing one of his gauntlets on the ground. The opponent would pick up the gauntlet to accept the challenge. Two men with swords would then face each other and fight it out, risking their lives until the offended person was satisfied or his opponent was dead. This is the artist's way of symbolizing the challenge that Patrick Henry is making to Great Britain an King George. Although Henry did not physically throw down a glove, his speech acted as a gauntlet.

Henry later apologized to the assembly and expressed his loyalty to the King. Nevertheless, the Resolves against the Stamp Act were adopted by a badly split House of Burgesses, and over the next few weeks were circulated through the colonies in various newspapers.

The fact that politicians in favor of the Crown quickly expunged the final resolutions from the record went largely unnoticed, and Virginia and Henry were widely extolled for their defense of American rights.

Henry's oratory stirred up the colonists, and many refused to pay the tax. Demonstrations against the British government were held in the streets of America, and the truth of Henry's argument "caught the conscience"* of William Pitt, the Elder, a renowned British statesman who was legendary for his oratory skills and the defense of liberty in the British Parliament.

As a member of the House of Commons in Britain, Pitt, a lover of Liberty, traveled to London from his sick bed to address the Parliament because he felt his love for liberty compelled him to join Henry and make a speech against the

Stamp Act. In Pitt's outspokenness against the Stamp Act, his fellow legislators accused him of encouraging rebellion against authority. Here is an excerpt from William Pitt's speech before Parliament, "In Defense of the Colonies":

William Pitt, the Elder

> Gentlemen, Sir, I have been charged with giving birth to sedition in America. *I believe the Americans* have spoken their sentiments with freedom against this unhappy act, and that freedom has become their crime. Sorry I am to hear that liberty of speech in this house is imputed as a crime. No gentleman should be afraid to exercise it ...

The gentleman tells us, America is obstinate; America is almost in open rebellion. I rejoice that America has resisted. Three million of people so dead to all feelings of liberty, as voluntarily to submit to be slaves, would have been fit instruments to make slaves of the rest. I come not here

---

* **From Shakespeare's Hamlet:** "The play's the thing, wherein I'll catch the conscience of the King." - This line was spoken by Hamlet, Prince of Denmark in the play *Hamlet*, written by William Shakespeare. After his father's death, Hamlet's Uncle Claudius became King and married his mother. Hamlet was told by a spirit who looked like his father that Hamlet's Uncle Claudius had murdered him by pouring poison in his ear. Hamlet devised a play in which he staged the murder of a king and invited his uncle to attend to see if his uncle's conscience would be pricked with guilt - thus proving the murder and the truth of the spirit's message.

armed at all points with law cases and acts of Parliament, with the statute book doubled down in dog-ears to defend the cause of liberty. If I had, I would have cited them to have shown that even under former arbitrary reigns, Parliaments were ashamed of taxing a people without their consent, and allowed them representatives ... The defense of liberty, upon a general principle, upon a constitutional principle, it is a ground on which I stand firm; on which I dare meet any man ...

I am no courtier of America; I stand up for this kingdom. I maintain, that the Parliament has a right to bind, to restrain America. Our legislative power over the colonies is sovereign and supreme. When it ceases to be sovereign and supreme, (*meaning the King should disregard Parliament and take absolute control*) I would advise every gentleman to sell his lands, if he can, and embark for that country. (*Colonies in America*)

When two countries are connected together, like England and her colonies, without being incorporated, the one must necessarily govern; the greater must rule the less; but so rule it, as not to contradict the fundamental principles that are common to both...

The gentleman asks, when were the colonies emancipated? But I desire to know, when were they made slaves ... The Americans have not acted in all things with prudence and temper. They have been wronged. They have been driven to madness by injustice ... Upon the whole, I will beg leave to tell the House what is really my opinion. It is, that the Stamp Act be repealed absolutely, totally, and immediately; that the reason for the repeal should be assigned, because it was founded on an erroneous principle ... and at the same time, let the sovereign authority of this country over the colonies be asserted in as strong terms as can be devised, and be made to extend to every point of legislation whatsoever: that we may bind their trade, confine their manufactures, and exercise every power whatsoever - except that of taking money out of their pockets without their consent.

Pitt agreed with Henry that it was unlawful to tax the colonists without the agreement of their representatives and believed that the Stamp Act should be repealed. It was - but in a strong show of who was still boss, Parliament immediately enacted the Declaratory Act. This Act stated that the British Parliament had power to bind the colonists in all points of trade to British regulation - a position Pitt agreed with, except on the issue of taxes. This "iron fist" attitude to rule the colonies was one of the last nails in the coffin that would bring on the war of so-called "rebellion."

While Pitt won the colonies freedom against the Stamp Ace, his last bit of advice to exercise absolute control over the businesses of the American colonies was the Achilles' heel that would bring down British rule. The idea of self-government, and the God-given right people have to "life, liberty, and the pursuit of happiness" was not yet understood in the world.

Patrick Henry's An Act of Treason - *Stamp Act Speech*: https://goo.gl/dLBv6W

The Speech that Finally Set the Ball Rolling

Soon after this, Patrick Henry would give what has come to be recognized as one of the greatest orations in world history. In March of 1775, Patrick Henry gave his *A Call to Arms* speech. This speech has been called "the world's most famous cry for freedom." Here is a portion of it:

Mr. President, it is natural for man to indulge in the illusions of hope. We are apt to shut our eyes against a painful truth, and listen to the song, till she transforms us into beasts. Is this the part of wise men, engaged in a great and arduous struggle for liberty? Are we disposed to be of the number of those, who, having eyes, see not, and having ears, hear not ...   *Bibel*

For my part, whatever anguish of spirit it may cost, I am willing to know the whole Truth; to know the worst, and to provide for it. I have but one lamp by which my feet are   *Bible* guided; and that is the lamp of experience. I know of no way of judging the future but by the past. And judging by the past, I wish to know what there has been in the conduct of the British ministry for the last ten years to justify those hopes ... Is it that insidious smile with which our petition has been lately received? Trust it not, sir; it will prove a snare to your feet. Suffer not yourselves to be betrayed with a kiss.   *Bible*

Ask yourselves how this gracious reception of our petition comports with those warlike preparations which cover our waters and darken our land. Are fleets and armies necessary to a work of love and reconciliation? Have we shown ourselves unwilling to be reconciled that force must be called in to win back our love? Let us not deceive ourselves, sir. These are the implements of war and subjugation; the last arguments to which kings resort.

I ask, gentlemen, what means this martial array, if its purpose be not to force us to submission? Can gentlemen assign any other possibility? Has Great Britain any enemy, in this quarter of the world, to call for all this accumulation of navies and armies? No, sir, she has none. They are meant for us: they can be meant for no other. They are sent over to bind and rivet to us those chains which the British ministry have been so long forging ... We have petitioned: we have remonstrated; we have supplicated; we have prostrated ourselves before the throne ... There is no longer any room for hope. If we wish to be free, if we mean to preserve inviolate those inestimable privileges for which we've been so long contending, if we mean not basely to abandon the noble struggle in which we have been so long engaged, and which we have pledged ourselves never to abandon until the glorious object of our contest shall be obtained, we must fight! I repeat it, sir, we must fight! An appeal to arms and to the God of Hosts is all that is left us!

They tell us that we are weak; unable to cope with so formidable an adversary. But when shall we be stronger? Will it be the next week, or the next year? Will it be when we are totally disarmed, and when a British guard shall be stationed in every house? Shall we gather strength by irresolution and inaction? ... Three millions of people, armed in the holy cause of liberty, and in such a country as that which we possess, are invincible by any force which our enemy can send against us.

Besides, Sir, we shall not fight our battles alone. There is a just God who presides over the destinies of nations, and who will raise up friends to fight our battles for us. The battle, Sir, is not to the strong alone; it is to the vigilant, the active, the brave ....

There is no retreat but in submission and slavery ... Our chains are forged! Their clanking may be heard on the plains of Boston! ... Is life so dear, or peace so sweet as to be purchased at the price of chains and slavery? Forbid it, Almighty God! I know not what course others may take, but as for me, give me liberty, or give me death!"

Watch the dramatization of Patrick Henry's "A Call to Arms": https://goo.gl/nXbMM7

Henry, The Effects of His Oratory

William Writ in his *Life of Patrick Henry* wrote the following account about the effect of Henry's *A Call to Arms Speech* on those who were present:

> He took his seat. No murmur of applause was heard. The effect was too deep. After the trance of a moment, several members started from their seats. The cry, "to arms!" seemed to quiver on every lip, and gleam from every eye. Richard H. Lee arose and supported Mr. Henry, with his usual spirit and elegance. But his melody was lost amid the agitations of that ocean, which the master-spirit of the storm had lifted up on high. That supernatural voice still sounded in their ears, and shivered along their arteries. They heard, in every pause, the cry of liberty or death. They became impatient of speech— their souls were on fire for action. [13]

Whose heart doesn't thrill at Patrick Henry's words as they echo down the corridors of time? Have you ever read this speech and wished that you could say even one line that was so stirring and so profound? Edward Carrington, who was listening outside a window of St. John's Church where this speech was delivered, was so moved by Henry's words that he asked to be buried at the spot - he was! George Mason, Founding Father and one of the Framers of the U.S. Constitution, wrote of the influence of Henry's oratory: "Every word Patrick Henry says not only engages but commands the attention, and your passions are no longer your own when he addresses them." [14]

Edmond Randolph wrote that after that speech was delivered, the convention sat in silence for several minutes. The rowdy round of applause and shouting that accompanies many speeches today is not always a sign that the audience has taken the point.

John Marshall, the son of Thomas Marshall, the first Chief Justice of the Supreme Court, said his father told him that Henry's speech was "one of the most bold, vehement, and animated pieces of eloquence that had ever been delivered." Henry did not write down this speech beforehand. Henry's speech, given impromptu, was the overflow of years of meditation and deliberation on the subject. The speech was written down by the listeners after it was delivered, to their best recollection. There is no doubt that his words lived on in the hearts of his hearers, a testimony to its source - Divine inspiration. The soldiers in the American Revolution all the way through the Civil War embroidered a slogan on their uniform that they made from

Flag of the Culpeper Virginia Minutemen - 1775

Henry's challenge - "Live Free or Die." Men and women may die, but Truth has the power to live on and continue to impact the heart and transform the world.

It is interesting to look behind the scenes to see just what influenced Henry's oratory skills. Henry was greatly impacted by the First Great Awakening and the fiery preaching of George Whitefield, Samuel Davies - known as the Evangelist of Virginia - and the camp meeting revivalists. Henry's mother was an avid participant in the revival meetings of the Awakening. At the age of thirteen, Patrick would hook up the horses to the wagon and take his mother to camp meetings where he listened with interest to the preaching. On the way back home his mother would ask him to re-preach the sermons to her, which he did with a lot of enthusiasm. This in essence was his training in oratory. Henry did not have formal schooling. He was home schooled by his father, who was a lawyer, and by his uncle, who was an Anglican preacher. He taught himself law and got three attorneys to sign for him so he could begin his practice.

Henry claimed that he was first taught what an orator should be by listening to the sermons of Samuel Davies. [15] (Never underestimate the importance of listening to good speakers.) Davies was one of early America's greatest preachers. His sermons had such a great impact in Virginia, but Davies spoke in London from time to time. Once while in London, he was invited to speak before King George II. Several times during his sermon the King whispered to those around him. Every time he did, Davies would pause until he was silent. Finally, Davies looked in the direction of King George and exclaimed, "When the lion roars, the beasts of the forest all tremble; and when King Jesus speaks, the princes of the earth should keep silence." [16] His remark was well-taken and the King sat in silence for the rest of Davies' message.

For the last eighteen months of his life, Davies was asked to take the post as the President of Princeton University and accepted so he could affect future preachers.

Following is a link to a text of one of Davies' speeches, "The Curse of Cowardice," delivered to the militia of Hanover County, Virginia, May 8, 1785. As you read this, you will see how much Davies' sentiments were impressed on the mind and spirit of the young Patrick Henry. You will notice the truth of Jesus' words when He reminded us, "The student who is fully trained will become like His teacher." (Luke 6:40)

Read the text of Samuel Davies' speech "The Curse of Cowardice" : https://goo.gl/deto2n

Re-enactment of Samuel Davies' speech, "What is it to be a Christian?" by Christian Praise: https://goo.gl/Kn6mhv

A Voice on Fire

When Henry's oratory skills burst forth on the national scene, it was because his heart was aflame with the ideas of liberty under God, and he knew what that meant. Henry "brought all the enthusiasm of the evangelistic Awakening to bear on the cause of freedom." [17] Historian Bernard Mayo writes about Henry's speeches: "His expressions seemed to have burned themselves into men's memories. Certainly, it was the spirit of that fiery orator who so powerfully influenced Virginians and events leading to American independence."[18]

Ten years before Patrick Henry's "Give me Liberty or give me death" proclamation, on May 29, 1765, Henry had given his famous oration against the Stamp Act. At that time there was a young man attending William and Mary College in Williamsburg, Virginia had taken a break from his intensive studies to hear the debates. He writes, "I attended the debate, standing at the door of the lobby of the House of Burgesses and heard the splendid display of Mr. Henry's talents as a popular orator. They were great indeed; such as I have never heard from any other man."

As the young man listened to Henry denounce the abuses against the American colonies, a flame began to kindle in his soul. Such a mighty surge of fervor for the cause of liberty raced through his entire being that the light from that flame burned brightly the rest of his life. The young man was Thomas Jefferson. He later referred to that day as the most important day of his life. It was the day that fixed his destiny.[19]

Thomas Jefferson called Patrick Henry the man "who set the ball of revolution rolling." Such is the power of anointed words that move the hearts of men. Certainly, Jefferson was influenced by Henry's sentiments expressed in his *Call to Arms* speech. We can hear their echo in the *Declaration of Independence*:

> In every stage of these Oppressions, We have Petitioned for Redress in the most humble terms: Our repeated Petitions have been answered only by repeated injury. A Prince, whose character is thus marked by every act which may define a Tyrant, is unfit to be the ruler of a free people...

> We, therefore, the Representatives of the United States of America, in General Congress, Assembled, appealing to the Supreme Judge of the world for the rectitude of our intentions, do, in the Name, and by Authority of the good People of these Colonies, solemnly publish and declare, That these united Colonies are, and of Right ought to be Free and Independent States...And for the support of this Declaration, with a firm reliance on the protection of Divine Providence, we mutually pledge to each other our Lives, our Fortunes, and our sacred Honor.

And what kind of faith that became the motivating factor of their lives did these two men have? Patrick Henry wrote, "It cannot be emphasized too strongly or too often that this great nation was founded, not by religionists, but by Christians; not on religions, but on the Gospel of Jesus Christ." [20]

Upon his death, the executors of his estate found a document among his Death Papers explaining the Virginia Resolutions and the events that led to America's separation from England. Then Henry wrote this, "Whether this will prove a blessing or a curse, will depend upon the use our people make of the blessings which a gracious God has bestowed upon us. If they are wise, they will be great and happy. If they are of a contrary character, they will be miserable. Righteousness alone can exalt them as a nation. Reader, whoever thou art, remember this; and in thy sphere, practice virtue thyself, and encourage it in others."

Thomas Jefferson wrote about himself, "I am a real Christian – that is to say, a disciple of the doctrines of Jesus Christ." [21] About the Bible, Jefferson reflected: "The Bible is the cornerstone of liberty... a student's perusal of the sacred volume will make us better citizens, better fathers, and better husbands." [22] Patrick Henry held the same sentiment. He wrote, "The Bible is worth all the other books which have ever been printed." [23]

Writing the Declaration of Independence
Thomas Jefferson, John Adams, Ben Franklin
by Jean Leon Jerome Ferris

(Take a look again at the front cover of this book at Rothermel's painting of Henry's Stamp Act Speech and you will see Thomas Jefferson in the balcony just above the letter p.)

John Adams - Founding Father, 2nd President of the United States, Spokesman for Liberty

Who cannot but be inspired by the words of John Adams when he cast his vote for the *Declaration of Independence*:

John Adams (1735-1826)
by Asher B. Durand

Sink or swim, live or die, survive or perish, I give my hand and my heart to this vote. It is true, indeed, that in the beginning we aimed not at independence. But there's a Divinity that shapes our ends ... Why then, should we defer the Declaration? ... We may die; die Colonists, die slaves, die - it may be ignominiously and on the scaffold. Be it so. Be it so. If it be the pleasure of Heaven that my country shall require the poor offering of my life, the victim shall be ready... But while I do live, let me have a country, or at least the hope of a country, and that a free country. But whatever may be our fate, be assured...that this Declaration will stand. It may cost treasure, and it may cost blood, but it will stand, and it will richly compensate for both.

Through the thick gloom of the present, I see the brightness of the future as the sun in heaven. We shall make this a glorious, an immortal day. When we are in our graves, our children will honor it.Before God, I believe the hour is come. My judgment approves this measure, and my whole heart is in it. All that I have, and all that I am, and all that I hope, in this life, I am now ready here to stake upon it; and I leave off as I began, that live or die, survive or perish, I am for the Declaration. It is my living sentiment, and by the blessing of God it shall be my dying sentiment. Independence now, and Independence forever!

Re-enactment of John Adams' speech on the Declaration of Independence: https://goo.gl/TyZX1a

Re-enactment of Declaration of Independence Read before the nation: https://goo.gl/gq9nyB

George Whitefield, Evangelist of the First Great Awakening

George Whitefield, one of the leaders of the First Great Awakening, was a contemporary of our Founding Fathers. Upon being barred from preaching in the churches in England, Whitefield responded by proclaiming, "The churches are closed, but bless God, the fields are open!" [24]

Whitefield moved his preaching to the open air where thousands of people gathered to hear him proclaim the Gospel - more than could have ever gathered in any church building. The result was the salvation of multiple thousands in England. He then moved to the American colonies.

It has been said that over eighty percent of the colonists heard Whitefield speak in person. He was such a powerful speaker that tens of thousands came to hear him speak in the open fields of the colonies without a microphone, and he could be heard by all. Here is an eyewitness account of one of his meetings:

Now it pleased God to send Mr. Whitefield into this land. I heard of his preaching at Philadelphia like one of the old apostles. Thousands flocked to hear him preach and great numbers were converted to Christ; I felt the Spirit of God drawing me by conviction.

Then one morning there came a messenger and said Mr. Whitefield was to preach this morning. I was in my field at work. I dropped my tool that I had in my hand and ran to my pasture for my horse with all my might, fearing that I should be too late to hear him.

I brought my horse home and soon mounted and took my wife up, and we went as fast as I thought the horse could bear. When my horse began to be out of breath, I would get down and put my wife on the saddle and bid her ride as fast as she could and not stop or slack for me except I bade her. So I would run until I was much out of breath, and then mount my horse again, and we went along as if we were fleeing for our lives. All the while we were fearing we should be too late, for we had twelve miles to ride double in little more than an hour.

When we came within about half a mile of the road, I heard a noise - something like a low rumbling thunder - and presently found it was the noise of horses coming down the road. A cloud of dust arose some rods into the air over the tops of the hills and trees. I heard no man speak a word, but everyone was pressing forward in great haste. Three or four thousand people assembled together. I turned and looked towards the great river and saw the ferry boats bringing loads of people; the land and banks by the river looked black with people and horses all along the twelve miles. I saw no man at work in his field, but all seemed to be gone. When I saw Mr. Whitefield come upon the scaffold, he looked almost angelical, a young, slim slender youth before some thousands of people, with a bold undaunted countenance. He looked as if he was clothed with authority from the Great God. And my hearing him preach gave me a heart wound; by God's blessing my old foundation was broken up, and I saw that my righteousness would not save me. [25]

Whitefield, The Effects of His Preaching

Although Whitefield was short in stature and cross-eyed, his words commanded multitudes. Benjamin Franklin took Whitefield as one of his closest friends. [26]   After one of Whitefield's revival meetings in Philadelphia, Franklin wrote about the effects of Whitefield's oratory and the power his words had to move the hearts of men: "There was a wonderful change soon made in the manners of our inhabitants. From being thoughtless or indifferent about religion, it seemed as if all the world were growing religious, so that one could not walk through the town in an evening without hearing psalms sung in different families of every street." [27]

Great Awakening Preacher Samuel Davies and his friend Gilbert Tennet once met Whitefield. Davies wrote about the effects of that meeting in his journal: "He spoke in the most encouraging manner as to the success of our mission, and in all his conversation discovered so much zeal and candor (*frank and*

honest), that I could not but admire the man as the wonder of the age! When we returned to our lodging, Mr. Tennent's heart was all on fire; and after we had gone to bed, he suggested that we should watch and pray, and we rose and prayed together till about 3 o'clock in the morning."[28]

Everyone in the colonies was familiar with Whitefield's famous story about his dream of going to heaven. Here it is: The first person Whitefield saw in heaven was Father Abraham. "Father Abraham," Whitefield asked, "whom have you in heaven? Any Episcopalians?" "No," Abraham answered. "Any Presbyterians?" "No," Father Abraham replied. "Have you any Independents or Seceders? "No," answered Abraham. "Have you any Methodists?" "No, No, No!" Father Abraham responded. "Whom have you here?" Whitefield asked in earnest. "We don't know those names here. All who are here are Christians - believers in Christ, those who have overcome by the blood of the Lamb and the word of their testimony." [29]

Whitefield's message helped end the strife and the persecution that was going on in the colonies between various Christian denominations. Whitefield's inspired oratory created a spirit of unity and brotherly love between the colonists and a determination to stand together, and regardless of denominational differences, to "stand fast in the liberty with which Christ had made *them* free and be not entangled again in the yoke of bondage" - the British oppression. Whitefield's preaching gave the colonists the Christian courage and unity they needed to work together for American Independence. Although the colonists differed on the right to own slaves and a great many of the Founding Fathers wanted to do away with slavery, they came to the conclusion that slavery was a battle for another generation to fight. Divine Providence had assigned them the task of overthrowing the belief in the rule of the Divine Right of Kings and establishing self-government among men.

Three

Great American Speakers
of the 19th Century

Elizabeth Cady Stanton - Champion of Women's Rights

Elizabeth Cady Stanton, abolitionist, social reformer, and founder of The National Women's Suffrage, is considered the true force behind the drive for equal rights for women in the United States. Although she died in 1902, before the passage of the Nineteenth Amendment to the Constitution that secured women's right to vote, Elizabeth Stanton worked tirelessly for fifty years to lay the groundwork for that reality.

Elizabeth Cady Stanton
(1815-1902)

In the documentary film, *Not for Ourselves Alone: The Story of Elizabeth Cady Stanton and Susan B. Anthony,* Ken Burns offers this commentary on the times in which Elizabeth Stanton lived: "In the middle of the nineteenth-century women were, by custom, barred from the pulpit and the professions, prevented from attending college and those who dared speak in public were thought indecent. By law, married women were prohibited from owning or inheriting property.   In fact, wives were the property of their husbands, who were entitled by law to her wages and her body." [30]

As a mother of seven children, Elizabeth worked tirelessly from home and wrote many of the speeches that her dear friend Susan B. Anthony delivered for her because Susan had the time to speak and travel since she was single and had no children. As a dedicated Christian, Elizabeth believed that the teachings of Christianity of that day did not reflect Jesus' view of women. This wrong teaching had resulted in women being treated as children, slaves, or property and had barred women from education, public speaking, and the opportunity to vote and participate in the political direction of the American Republic.

Elizabeth writes that when she was eleven, her brother Eleazar died. She watched her father sitting before the casket in their parlor grieving for a long time. She climbed into his lap and threw her arms around him and put her head upon his chest and tried to comfort him. After a while, her father tearfully responded, "Oh, my daughter, I wish you were a boy!" This experience had a profound effect on Elizabeth, and she resolved to be everything to her father that her brother had been. That meant to her she needed to give up play and to be learned and courageous.

Elizabeth went to their neighbor, Rev. Simon Hosack, for spiritual advice and asked him if he liked boys or girls best. When he answered, "I like girls best!" she told him of her decision and asked if he would help her learn Greek. She writes, "He entered fully into the feeling of suffering and sorrow which took possession of me when I discovered that a girl weighed less in the scale of being than a boy, and he praised my determination to prove the contrary." [31]

Rev. Hosack encouraged her to read widely and ultimately bequeathed to her his own Greek Lexicon along with other books. His confirmation of her endeavors strengthened Elizabeth's confidence. Unlike many women of her era, Elizabeth Stanton was formally educated. Although her father was not that keen on women's education, she was encouraged in intellectual pursuits by Rev. Hosack. Elizabeth attended Johnstown Academy until she was sixteen where she studied Latin, Greek, French, mathematics, religion, science, and writing.

At the Academy, she enjoyed being in co-educational classes where she could compete intellectually and academically with boys her age and older. She did this very successfully, winning several academic awards and honors, including the award for Greek language. Since women were barred from men's colleges in 1830, Elizabeth attended Troy Female Seminary where she was influenced by its founder Emma Willard. [32] This was the first institution of serious learning for young women in the United States.

Elizabeth Stanton, Abolitionist, Speaker and Organizer of the First Women's Rights Convention

Elizabeth worked tirelessly in the abolitionist movement. While visiting her cousin, she met her husband Henry Stanton, an abolitionist lecturer and founding member of the New York Anti-Slavery Society. As an active abolitionist, Elizabeth, newly married, accompanied her husband to the World Anti-Slavery Convention in London.

There were many women who had been sent to the convention from different places in the world, and yet she and all the other women who had come were not allowed to attend. The convention refused to seat them as delegates because they were women. Her husband made an impassioned speech to allow the women equal entrance, but to no avail. English prejudices, at that time, held that women were excluded by Scriptural texts from sharing equal dignity and authority with men in all reform associations. For all the women who had come so far to attend and who had worked so tirelessly for abolition, the experience was a bitter pill to swallow. The determination of the spiritual leaders of the convention to keep half of the human race silent, forbidden both to speak and vote, was to Elizabeth totally against the tenet of Scriptures which proclaimed, "Where the Spirit of the Lord is there is liberty!" This attitude relegated women themselves to slavery to men. This was an offense that Elizabeth could not allow to stand unchallenged.

Elizabeth was so outraged that when she returned home, she co-organized the 1848 Women's Rights Convention in Seneca Falls, New York, where her presentation speech garnered her credit for initiating the first organized women's rights and women's suffrage movements in the United States. [33] After her seven children were grown, Elizabeth dedicated eight months out of every year to speaking and spreading her ideas. Here is a portion of the address she gave to the First Women's Rights Convention, July 19,1848:

> We are assembled to protest against a form of government existing without the consent of the governed - to declare our right to be free as man is free, to be represented in the government which we are taxed to support, to have such disgraceful laws as give man the power to chastise and imprison his wife, to take the wages which she earns, the property which she inherits, and, in case of separation, the children of her love; laws which make her the mere dependent on his bounty. It is to protest against such unjust laws as these that we are assembled today, and to have them, if possible, forever erased from our statute books, deeming

them a shame and a disgrace to a Christian republic in the nineteenth-century.

We have met to uplift woman's fallen divinity upon an even pedestal with man's. And, strange as it may seem to many, we now demand our right to vote according to the Declaration of the government under which we live. This right no one pretends to deny. We need not prove ourselves equal to Daniel Webster to enjoy this privilege, for the ignorant Irishman in the ditch has all the civil rights he has. We need not prove our muscular power equal to this same Irishman to enjoy this privilege, for the most tiny, weak, ill-shaped

stripling of twenty-one has all the civil rights of the Irishman ...

All white men in this country have the same rights, however they may differ in mind, body, or estate. The right is ours. The question now is: how shall we get possession of what rightfully belongs to us? ... to have drunkards, idiots, horse-racing, rum-selling rowdies, ignorant foreigners, and silly boys fully recognized, while we ourselves are thrust out from all the rights that belong to citizens, it is too grossly insulting to the dignity of woman to be longer quietly submitted to. The right is ours. Have it, we must. Use it, we will. The pens, the tongues, the fortunes, the indomitable wills of many women are already pledged to secure this right. The great truth that no just government can be formed without the consent of the governed we shall echo and re-echo in the ears of the unjust judge, until by continual coming we shall weary him.

There seems now to be a kind of moral stagnation in our midst. Philanthropists have done their utmost to rouse the nation to a sense of its sins. War, slavery, drunkenness, licentiousness, gluttony have been dragged naked before the people, and all their abominations and deformities fully brought to light, yet with idiotic laugh we hug those monsters to our breasts and rush on to destruction. Our churches are multiplying on all sides, our missionary societies, Sunday schools, and prayer meetings and innumerable charitable and reform organizations are all in operation, but still the tide of vice is swelling, and threatens the destruction of everything, and the battlements of righteousness are weak against the raging elements of sin and death.

Verily, the world waits the coming of some new element, some purifying power, some spirit of mercy and love. The voice of woman has been silenced in the state, the church, and the home, but man cannot fulfill his destiny alone, he cannot redeem his race unaided. There are deep and tender chords of sympathy and love in the hearts of the downfallen and oppressed that woman can touch more skillfully than man.

The world has never yet seen a truly great and virtuous nation, because in the degradation of woman the very fountains of life are poisoned at their source. It is vain to look for silver and gold from mines of copper and lead. It is the wise mother that has the wise son. So long as your women are slaves you may throw your colleges and churches to the winds. You can't have scholars and saints so long as your mothers are ground to powder between the upper and nether millstone of tyranny and lust. How seldom, now, is a father's pride gratified, his fond hopes realized, in the budding genius of his son! The wife is degraded, made the mere creature of caprice, and the foolish son is heaviness to his heart. Truly are the sins of the fathers visited upon the children to the third and fourth generation.

God, in His wisdom, has so linked the whole human family together that any violence done at one end of the chain is felt throughout its length, and here, too, is the law of restoration, as in woman all have fallen, so in her elevation shall the race be recreated. "Voices" were the visitors and advisers of Joan of Arc. Do not "voices" come to us daily from the haunts of poverty, sorrow, degradation, and despair, already too long unheeded.

Now is the time for the women of this country, if they would save our free institutions, to defend the right to buckle on the armor that can best resist the keenest weapons of the enemy - contempt and ridicule. The same religious enthusiasm that nerved Joan of Arc to her work nerves us to ours.

In every generation God calls some men and women for the utterance of truth, a heroic action, and our work today is the fulfilling of what has long since been foretold by the Prophet - Joel 2:28: "And it shall come to pass afterward, that I will pour out my spirit upon all flesh; and your sons and your daughters shall prophesy."

We do not expect our path will be strewn with the flowers of popular applause, but over the thorns of bigotry and prejudice will be our way, and on our banner will beat the dark storm clouds of opposition from those who have entrenched themselves behind the stormy bulwarks of custom and authority, and who have fortified their position by every means, holy and unholy. But we will steadfastly abide the result. Unmoved, we will bear it aloft. Undauntedly we will unfurl it to the gale, for we know that the storm cannot rend from it a shred, that the electric flash will but more clearly show to us the glorious words inscribed upon it, "Equality of Rights."

Elizabeth Offers a New Look at the Word of God

Elizabeth Cady Stanton with Two of Her Children, Daniel and Henry

Source: Library of Congress

To give people the opportunity to see traditional views of women in a different light, Elizabeth and a committee of 26 women wrote a commentary on the Bible called *The Woman's Bible,* which was published in 1895. While Elizabeth's views on women have for the most part been embraced in most Western nations today, they were very controversial when she presented them and are still controversial among some religious sects and in many parts of the world. Elizabeth believed that Jesus had great compassion for women and addressed this issue in His parable about the five wise virgins who had oil in their lamps and went into the wedding feast, while the five foolish virgins were not able to go in because they let the oil in their lamps run out.

Elizabeth believed that part of being able to understand the deeper meaning of this parable lay in the relationship the parable of the virgins held to the two parables that followed it in Scripture. In these parables Jesus points out that there will be rewards and punishments for the way we live. The parable of the virgins is followed by the parable of the distribution of talents, which concludes with the reward for the stewards who used what the master had given them wisely and the punishment for the one who did not. The parable of the talents is followed by the parable of the sheep and goats. Those who did something with their lives to help others Jesus calls the "sheep" and those who did not aid others, Jesus labeled the "goats." The "sheep" entered into everlasting reward, but the "goats" were sent into everlasting punishment of eternal fire.

The fact that these parables were grouped together was evidence to Elizabeth that she was taking the meaning correctly and that all three parables emphasized the truth that failure to use and improve your God-given gifts and talents in life and failure to help others ended in loss and eternal judgment. That Jesus mentioned in the parables both men and women, was evidence enough that regardless of the societal norms of that day, women were not exempt from taking responsibility for the way they lived. Here are Elizabeth's comments on this parable. (Matt. 25:1-12)

In this chapter we have the duty of self-development impressively and repeatedly urged in the form of parables, addressed alike to man and to woman. The sin of neglecting and of burying one's talents, capacities and powers, and the penalties which such a course involve, are here strikingly portrayed.

This parable of the virgins waiting for the wedding feast is found among the Jewish records substantially the same as in our own Scriptures. Their weddings were generally celebrated at night; yet they usually began at the rising of the evening star; but in this case there was a more than ordinary delay. Adam Clarke in his commentaries explains this parable as referring chiefly to spiritual gifts and the religious life. He makes the Lord of Hosts the bridegroom, the judgment day the wedding feast, the foolish virgins the sinners whose hearts were cold and dead, devoid of all spiritual graces, and unfit to enter the kingdom of heaven. The wise virgins were the saints who were ready for translation, or for the bridal procession. They followed to the wedding feast; and when the chosen had entered "the door was shut."

This strikes us as a strained interpretation of a very simple parable, which, considered in connection with the other parables, seems to apply much more closely to this life than to that which is to come, to the intellectual and the moral nature, and to the whole round of human duties. It fairly describes the two classes which help to make up society in general.

The ones who, like the foolish virgins, have never learned the first important duty of cultivating their own individual powers, using the talents given to them, and keeping their own lamps trimmed and burning. The idea of being a helpmeet to somebody else has been so sedulously drilled into most women that an individual life, aim, purpose and ambition are never taken into consideration. They of times do so much in other directions that they neglect the most vital duties to themselves.

We may find in this simple parable a lesson for the cultivation of courage and of self-reliance. These virgins are summoned to the discharge of an important duty at midnight, alone, in darkness, and in solitude. No chivalrous gentleman is there to run for oil and to trim their lamps. They must depend on themselves, unsupported, and pay the penalty of their own improvidence and unwisdom. Perhaps in that bridal procession might have been seen fathers, brothers, friends, for whose service and amusement the foolish virgins had wasted many precious hours, when they should have been trimming their own lamps and keeping oil in their vessels.

And now, with music, banners, lanterns, torches, guns and rockets fired at intervals, come the bride and the groom, with their attendants and friends numbering thousands, brilliant in jewels, gold and silver, magnificently mounted on richly caparisoned horses - for nothing can be more brilliant than were those nuptial solemnities of Eastern nations. As this spectacle, grand beyond description, sweeps by, imagine the foolish virgins pushed aside, in the shadow of some tall edifice, with dark, empty lamps in their hands, unnoticed and unknown.

And while the castle walls resound with music and merriment, and the lights from every window stream out far into the darkness, no kind friends gather round them to sympathize in their humiliation, nor to cheer their loneliness. It matters little that women may be ignorant, dependent, unprepared for trial and for temptation. Alone they must meet the terrible emergencies of life, to be sustained and protected amid danger and death by their own courage, skill and self-reliance, or perish. ...

It is not commendable for the women of this Republic to expend much enthusiasm on political parties as now organized, nor in national celebrations, for they have as yet no lot or part in the great experiment of self-government. In their ignorance, women sacrifice themselves to educate the men of their households, and to make of themselves ladders by which their husbands, brothers and sons climb up into the kingdom of knowledge, while they themselves are shut out from all intellectual companionship, even with those they love best; such are indeed like the foolish virgins.

Derelicta *by* Botticelli

They have not kept their own lamps trimmed and burning; they have no oil in their vessels, no resources in themselves; they bring no light to their households nor to the circle in which they move; and when the bridegroom cometh, when the philosopher, the scientist, the saint, the scholar, the great and the learned, all come together to celebrate the marriage feast of science and religion, the foolish virgins, though present, are practically shut out; for what know they of the grand themes which inspire each tongue and kindle every thought? Even the brothers and the sons whom they have educated, now rise to heights which they cannot reach, span distances which they cannot comprehend. The solitude of ignorance, oh, who can measure its misery! The wise virgins are they who keep their lamps trimmed, who burn oil in their vessels for their own use, who have improved every advantage for their education, secured a healthy, happy, complete development, and entered all the profitable avenues of labor, for self-support, so that when the opportunities and the responsibilities of life come, they may be fitted fully to enjoy the one and ably to discharge the other.

These are the women who today are close upon the heels of man in the whole realm of thought, in art, in science, in literature and in government. With telescopic vision they explore the starry firmament, and bring back the history of the planetary world. With chart and compass they pilot ships across the mighty deep, and with skillful fingers send electric messages around the world. In galleries of art, the grandeur of nature and the greatness of humanity are immortalized by them on canvas, and by their inspired touch, dull blocks of marble are transformed into angels of light.

In music, they speak again the language of Mendelssohn, of Beethoven, of Chopin, of Schumann, and are worthy interpreters of their great souls. The poetry and the novels of the century are theirs; they, too, have touched the keynote of reform in religion, in politics and in social life. They fill the editors' and the professors' chairs, plead at the bar of justice, walk the wards of the hospital, and speak from the pulpit and the platform.

Such is the widespread preparation for the marriage feast of science and religion; such is the type of womanhood which the bridegroom of an enlightened public sentiment welcomes today; and such is the triumph of the wise virgins over the folly, the ignorance and the degradation of the past as in grand procession they enter the temple of knowledge, and the door is no longer shut. [34]

Results of Elizabeth Cady Staton's Oratory

Elizabeth recognized the important connection between abolition and women's rights in a speech she gave before the American Anti-Slavery Society:

> Yes, this is the only organization on God's footstool where the humanity of woman is recognized, and these are the only men who have ever echoed back her cries for justice and equality....the mission of the Radical Anti-Slavery Movement is not to the African slave alone, but to the slaves of custom, creed, and sex, as well, and most faithfully has it done its work.

In 1860, Elizabeth enjoyed a victory after working so tirelessly on the issue of married women's rights. The New York Legislature enacted the Married Women's Property Law of 1860, giving "married women the right to own property, engage in business, manage their wages and other income, sue and be sued, and be joint guardian of their children." These rights would eventually be acknowledged and protected in every other state in the Union.[35]   A few years later, Elizabeth enjoyed the victory of her work in the abolitionist movement - the overthrow of slavery in the United States.

Elizabeth gave voice to Truth that forever changed the American landscape in scope and vision, both in the abolition of slavery and her fight for women's rights - the right to vote, the right to participate in the offices of our Republic, the right to own property, the right of women to be the guardians of their children, the right to speak publicly, the right to work in the professions, and the right of women to acquire an education.

After her death, Elizabeth's ideas to give women equal rights were eventually codified into law - proving the fact that generations may come and go, but Truth lives on and "goes forth, conquering and to conquer." When we preach the Truth, it will accomplish the task that God sent it to do. The results may seem to be long in coming, but the ax has been laid to the root, and one day the oppressive edifice that fights against the will of God and the blessing of humankind will come down in one grand crash.

This has been happening since Jesus our Savior and the God of heaven set up a kingdom that cannot be destroyed. Jesus promised this to His disciples long ago, "Upon this rock of the revelation of who I am, I will establish the *culture of heaven* (also translated the *ecclessia* or my *church*) and the gates of hell will not be able to prevail against it or overpower it." (Matt. 16:18)

What was the source of Elizabeth's inspired oratory? She tells us in her own words:

> They tell us sometimes that if we had only kept quiet, all these desirable things would have come about of themselves. I am reminded of the Greek clown who, having seen an archer bring down a flying bird, remarked,

sagely: 'You might have saved your arrow, for the bird anyway would have been killed by the fall.'[36] The moment we begin to fear the opinions of others and hesitate to tell the truth that is in us, and from motives of policy are silent when we should speak, the Divine floods of Light and Life no longer flow into our souls.[37]

Abraham Lincoln, President of the United States, Orator, Liberator

Abraham Lincoln
16th President of the United States

The preachers of the Second Great Awakening, Harriet Beecher Stowe, author of *Uncle Tom's Cabin*, and all the members of the Abolitionists' Movement created the spiritual climate for the overthrow of slavery. England had made slavery illegal by a long struggle in Parliament led by dynamic Christian statesman, William Wilberforce. The lot to end slavery in the United States fell upon Abraham Lincoln. Many saw the Civil War as God's judgment against slavery. President Abraham Lincoln as well eventually came to see it as this. During the dark days of the Civil War, he spoke immortal words in his *Second Inaugural Address* which would later be etched in stone on the walls of the Lincoln Memorial. His oratory in this address could be equated to biblical prophecy and is known as the greatest speech in American history. Here is a portion of that speech which explains what he believed to be the meaning of the Civil War:

One-eighth of the whole population were colored slaves, not distributed generally over the Union, but localized in the southern part of it. These slaves constituted a peculiar and powerful interest. All knew that this interest was somehow the cause of the war... Both parties deprecated war, but one of them would make war rather than let the nation survive, and the other would accept war rather than let it perish, and the war came... It may seem strange that any men should dare to ask a just God's assistance in wringing their bread from the sweat of other men's faces, but let us judge not, that we be not judged. The prayers of both could not be answered. That of neither has been answered fully. The Almighty has His own purposes. "Woe unto the world because of offenses; for it must needs be that offenses come, but woe to that man by whom the offense cometh."

If we shall suppose that American slavery is one of those offenses which, in the providence of God, must needs come, but which, having continued through His appointed time, He now wills to remove, and that He gives to both North and South this terrible war as the woe due to those by whom the offense came, shall we discern therein any departure from those divine attributes which the believers in a living God always ascribe to Him? Fondly do we hope, fervently do we pray, that this mighty scourge of war may speedily pass away. Yet, if God wills that it continue until all the wealth piled by the bondman's two hundred and fifty years of unrequited toil be sunk, and until every drop of blood drawn with the lash shall be paid by another drawn with the sword, as was said three thousand years ago, so still it must be said, "The judgments of the Lord are true and righteous altogether."

With malice toward none; with charity for all; with firmness in the right, as God gives us to see the right, let us strive on to finish the work we are in; to bind up the nation's wounds; to care for him who shall have borne the battle, and for his widow, and his orphan—to do all which may achieve and cherish a just, and a lasting peace, among ourselves, and with all nations.

Writing about the effect of this speech on those who heard it, Father Charles Chiniquiy, a former Catholic priest and close friend of Lincoln, wrote:

These sublime words, falling from the lips of the greatest Christian whom God ever put at the head of a nation, only a few days before his martyrdom, sent a thrill of wonder through the whole world. The God-fearing people and the upright of every nation listened to them as if they had just come from the golden harp of David. Even the infidels remained mute with admiration and awe. It seemed to all that the echoes of heaven and earth were repeating that last hymn, falling from the heart of the noblest and truest Gospel man of our days. [38]

Lincoln's Second Inaugural Address: https://goo.gl/eSssJm

An Analysis of Second Inaugural: https://goo.gl/g3C1wK

Lincoln, His Faith

And what of Lincoln's faith? What motivating factor was at the heart of Lincoln's oratorical eloquence? Newton Bateman, Superintendent of Public Instruction for the State of Illinois and a personal friend of the President, shares this visit he had with Lincoln:

Mr. Lincoln paused, his features surcharged with emotion. Then he rose and walked up and down the reception room, in the effort to retain or regain his self-possession. Stopping at last, he said, with a trembling voice and his cheeks wet with tears: "I know there is a God, and that He hates injustice and slavery. I see the storm coming and I know that His hand is in it. If He has a place and work for me, and I think He has, I believe I am ready! I am nothing, but Truth is everything! I know I am right, because I know that liberty is right: for Christ teaches it, and Christ is God. I have told them that a house divided against itself cannot stand, and Christ and reason say the same thing, and they will find it so. Douglas does not care whether slavery is voted up or down. But God cares, and humanity cares, and I care.

And with God's help, I will not fail. I may not see the end, but it will come, and I shall be vindicated; and those men will see that they have not read their Bible right! Does it not appear strange that men can ignore the moral aspect of this contest? A revelation could not make it plainer to me that slavery, or the Government, must be destroyed. The future would be something awful, as I look at it, but for this Rock on which I stand (alluding to the Gospel book he still held in his hand). It seems as if God had borne with slavery until the very teachers of religion had come to defend it from the Bible, and to claim for it a Divine character and sanction. And now the cup of iniquity is full, and the vials of wrath will be poured out." [39]

During the Civil War President Lincoln was warned on many occasions of plots to assassinate him. On one such occasion, Lincoln was warned by his friend Father Chiniquy that the Vatican* had a plot to take his life. Lincoln said,

"You are not the first to warn me against the dangers of assassination. My ambassadors in Italy, France, and England, as well as Professor Morse, have many times warned me against the plots of the murderers which they have detected in those different countries. But I see no other safeguard against those murderers but to be always ready to die, as Christ advises ..."

Then he opened his Bible to the third chapter of Deuteronomy, and read from the 22nd to the 28th verse: "Let me tell you that I have lately read a passage in the Old Testament which has made a profound, and, I hope, a salutary impression on me. Here is that passage: 'You shall not fear them: for the Lord your God, He shall fight for you.' And I besought the Lord at that time, saying, 'O Lord God, You have begun to show Your servant Your greatness and Your mighty hand; for what God is there, in heaven or in earth, that can do according to Your works, and according to Your might! I pray, let me go over, and see the good land that is beyond Jordan, that goodly mountain, and Lebanon.'

" 'But the Lord was angry with me for your sakes, and would not hear me: and the Lord said unto me, 'Let it be enough for you: speak no more to Me of this matter. Get up into the top of Pisgah* and lift up your eyes westward and northward and southward and eastward, and behold it with your eyes, for you shall not cross over the Jordan.' "

After the President had read these words with great solemnity, he added:

"My dear Father Chiniquy, let me tell you that I have read these strange and beautiful verses several times these last five or six weeks. The more I read them, the more it seems to me that God has written them for me as well as for Moses ... It seems to me that the Lord wants, today, as He wanted in the days of Moses, another victim - a victim which He has himself chosen, anointed and prepared for the sacrifice, by raising it above the rest of His people. I cannot conceal from you that my impression is that I am that victim.

"Now, I see the end of this terrible conflict, with the same joy of Moses, when, he was at the end of his trying forty years in the wilderness. I prayed to my God to grant me to see the days of peace, and untold prosperity, which will follow this cruel war, as Moses asked God to see the other side of Jordan and enter the Promised Land. But do you know that I hear in my soul, as the voice of God, giving me the rebuke which was given to Moses?

"Why did God Almighty refuse to grant Moses the favor of crossing the Jordan, and entering the Promised Land? It was on account of his own nation's sins! That law of divine retribution and justice, by which one must suffer for another, is surely a terrible mystery.

"When I look on Moses, alone, silently dying on the Mount Pisgah,* I see that law, in one of its most sublime human manifestations, and I am filled with admiration and awe. But when I consider that law of justice, and expiation in the death of the Just, the Divine Son of Mary, on the mountain of Calvary, I remain mute in my adoration. The spectacle of that crucified one which is before my eyes, is more than sublime, it is divine! Moses died for his people's sake, but Christ died for the whole world's sake! Both died to fulfill the same eternal law of the divine justice, though in a different measure. But my fear is that the justice of God is not yet paid. "When I look upon the rivers of tears and blood drawn by the lashes of the merciless masters from the veins of the

---

* Pisgah - a Prophetic Note: President Lincoln said this in 1862. Lincoln was assassinated in 1865. The last shot of the Civil War was fired in 1865 from what is now Waynesville, N.C., twenty miles from what is now Waynesville, N.C., twenty miles from Mt. Pisgah, North Carolina. The mountain took its name from the mountain Moses spoke of in this passage.

very heart of those millions of defenseless slaves, these two hundred years, when I remember the agonies, the cries, the unspeakable tortures of those unfortunate people, at which I have, to some extent, connived with so many others for a part of my life, I feel that we are still far from the complete expiation. For the judgments of God are true and righteous. "But just as the Lord heard no murmur from the lips of Moses when He told him that he had to die before crossing the Jordan for the sins of his people; so I hope and pray that He will hear no murmur from me when I fall for my nation's sake."

Never had I heard such sublime words: Never had I seen a human face so solemn and so prophet-like as the face of the President, when uttering these things. Every sentence had come to me as a hymn from heaven, reverberated by the echoes of the mountains of Pisgah and Calvary. I was beside myself. Bathed in tears, I tried to say something, but I could not utter a word.[40]

Lincoln's Secret

What was the secret of Lincoln's oratory? Father Chiniquy offered the following explanation:

Every time I met President Lincoln, I wondered how such elevation of thought and such childish simplicity could be found in the same man. After my interviews with him many times, I said to myself: "How can this rail-splitter have so easily raised himself to the highest range of human thought and philosophy?"

The secret of this was that Lincoln had spent a great part of his life at the school of Christ, and that he meditated on His sublime teachings to an extent unsuspected by the world. I found in him the most perfect type of Christianity I ever met. Professedly, he was neither a strict Presbyterian, nor a Baptist, nor a Methodist; but he was the embodiment of all which is more perfect and Christian in them. His religion was the very essence of what God wants in man. It was from Christ Himself he had learned to love God and his neighbor, as it was from Christ he had learned the dignity and the value of man. "Ye are all brethren, the children of God," was his great motto.

It was from the Gospel that he had learned his principles of equality, fraternity, and liberty, as it was from the Gospel he had learned that sublime, childish simplicity which, alone, and forever, won the admiration and affection of all those who approached him.[41]

What was the result of Lincoln's bold stand against slavery? Not only was slavery overthrown in the United States, slavery, a practice as old as the human race that was defended as right and good by many Christians, was eradicated from being an acceptable practice forever. Does slavery still exist somewhere in the world? Yes, in the darkness of organized crime or unenlightened oppressive regimes. This will eventually change. But among the civilized nations of the world, the buying and selling of men, women and children - once common place - is considered, immoral, unethical and illegal.

*Vatican - Historic Note: In Europe, the Protestant Reformation was the result of devout Catholics trying to reform the Catholic Church according to the teachings of the Bible which had just been made available to the masses because of invention of the printing press. This reform was rejected by the Catholic Church and many people left the Church to conform their lives to Biblical teaching. The Kings of England and Holland separated their nations from the Catholic Church and withdrew their allegiance to the Pope. Many wars were fought in Europe by both France and Spain to bring

England and Holland back under the control of the Pope and restore Papal control over all the European Kings. ThoseProtestants who wanted more reformation than the King of England or other reformed state churches of Europe would allow were persecuted by these state churches. Because of persecution, Protestants fled Europe to seek religious freedom in North America. Nevertheless, the French Jesuits tried to found colonies in the New World. They established a colony in Quebec and from there stirred up the Indians to slaughter the British colonists in America to try to bring the New World under French control and give the Catholic Church the dominion and control it sought. This was known as the French and Indian Wars. Colonists were mercilessly slaughtered by Indian attacks for over 150 years. The King of France finally got tired of the war that he was fighting on behalf of the Pope, gave up, and was defeated by the British.

However, the Papacy continued to try to recover from the mortal wound it received during the Protestant Reformation. The Papacy made attempts to try to divide the United States and support the Confederacy. Jefferson Davis, the President of the Confederacy, was a Catholic and was called by the Pope, "My dear son." Besides being warned of assignation attempts spawned by the Vatican, President Lincoln had a prophetic word about the Papacy and its interference in this country. He remarked to Father Chiniquy that while the Papacy's attempts to destroy our nation had been great, he believed that this War marked the end of the Papacy's interference in our nation. His prophecy came true. In 1870, five years after the Civil War, Italy waged war with the Vatican States and re-annexed all of them to Italy. This ended the Pope's status as a titular head of a nation and ended his standing army and his political power. The Vatican remained a part of Italy until 1929, when Vatican City - 110 acres - was authorized as a sovereign city-state by the Italian government.

Lincoln's historic stand against slavery:
https://goo.gl/LN4mqs

Four

Great American Speakers
of the 20th Century

Martin Luther King, Pastor and Civil Rights Leader

Over one hundred years later, Dr. Martin Luther King, Baptist preacher and Civil Rights leader picked up Elizabeth Cady Stanton's cry for equal rights. In his *Letter from the Birmingham Jail*, Dr. King writes to the religious leaders of Birmingham, Alabama, who are opposing the civil rights demonstration held there. King expounds on Stanton's theme that it is a false notion that time alone will bring changes. Here is a short excerpt.

Dr. Martin Luther King
National Archives

One of the basic points in your statement is that the action that I and my associates have taken in Birmingham is untimely. Lamentably, it is an historical fact that privileged groups seldom give up their privileges voluntarily. Individuals may see the moral light and voluntarily give up their unjust posture; but, as Reinhold Niebuhr has reminded us, groups tend to be more immoral than individuals.

We know through painful experience that freedom is never voluntarily given by the oppressor; it must be demanded by the oppressed. Frankly, I have yet to engage in a direct-action campaign that was "well timed" in the view of those who have not suffered unduly from the disease of segregation. For years now I have heard the word "Wait!" It rings in the ear of every Negro with piercing familiarity.

This "Wait" has almost always meant "Never." We must come to see, with one of our distinguished jurists, that "justice too long delayed is justice denied." We have waited for more than 340 years for our constitutional and God-given rights. ... When you go forever fighting a degenerating sense of "nobodiness" then you will understand why we find it difficult to wait. There comes a time when the cup of endurance runs over, and men are no longer willing to be plunged into the abyss of despair. I hope, sirs, you can understand our legitimate and unavoidable impatience. ...

But though I was initially disappointed at being categorized as an extremist, as I continued to think about the matter I gradually gained a measure of satisfaction from the label. Was not Jesus an extremist for love. ... Was not Paul an extremist for the Christian gospel: "I bear in my body the marks of the Lord Jesus."

Was not Martin Luther an extremist: "Here I stand; I cannot do otherwise, so help me God." And John Bunyan: "I will stay in jail to the end of my days before I make a butchery of my conscience." And Abraham Lincoln: "This nation cannot survive half slave and half free." And Thomas Jefferson: "We hold these truths to be self-evident, that all men are created equal."... So the question is not whether we will be extremists, but what kind of extremists we will be. Will we be extremists for hate or for love? Will we be extremists for the preservation of injustice or for the extension of justice? ...

There was a time when the church was very powerful in the time when the early Christians rejoiced at being deemed worthy to suffer for what they believed. In those days the church was not merely a thermometer that recorded the ideas and principles of popular opinion; it was a thermostat that transformed the mores of society.

Whenever the early Christians entered a town, the people in power became disturbed and immediately sought to convict the Christians for being "disturbers of the peace" and "outside agitators." But the Christians pressed on, in the conviction that they were "a colony of heaven," called to obey God rather than man. Small in number, they were big in commitment. They were too God intoxicated to be "astronomically intimidated."...

Things are different now. So often the contemporary church is a weak, ineffectual voice with an uncertain sound. So often it is an arch defender of the status quo. Far from being disturbed by the presence of the church, the power structure of the average community is consoled by the church's silent and often even vocal sanction of things as they are. ...

If today's church does not recapture the sacrificial spirit of the early church, it will lose its authenticity, forfeit the loyalty of millions, and be dismissed as an irrelevant social club with no meaning...

Dr. King's speech from Letter from Birmingham Jail
https://goo.gl/f3SVgR

Dr. King's Speech that Changed History

Dr. King Delivers His *I Have a Dream* **Speech**
Lincoln Memorial, August 28, 1963 - Associated Press

August 28, 1963, during the Civil Rights Movement, Dr. King delivered his world-famous *I Have a Dream* speech on the steps of the Lincoln Memorial, at the *March on Washington for Jobs and Freedom* rally. The speech has great historical significance and is seen as a turning point in the struggle for equality for African Americans. The speech has been ranked among the one hundred greatest historic speeches of all time by top scholars and speech writers.

In the middle of Dr. King's speech, noted black gospel singer Mahalia Jackson, who had sung earlier in the event, shouted to Dr. King from the crowd, "Tell them about the dream, Martin."[42] Dr. King stopped delivering his prepared speech and started "preaching," moving out into the realms of God's Eternal Spirit. Jesus promised, when you stand before leaders and councils, the Holy Spirit at that moment will give you what you are to say.

Even journalists reported that Something greater than Dr. King took over that day. Marquis Childs of *The Washington Post* wrote that King's speech "rose above mere oratory."[43] *The Los Angeles Times* reported that Dr. King displayed "matchless eloquence" and was "a supreme orator" of "a type so rare as almost to be forgotten in our age." *The Times* reported that Dr. King put to shame the advocates of segregation by inspiring the "conscience of America" with the justice of the civil-rights cause.[44] His speech still has the power to stir hearts today. Here is a short excerpt of Dr. King's *I have a Dream* speech.

> I am not unmindful that some of you have come here out of great trials and tribulations. Some of you have come fresh from narrow jail cells. Some of you have come from areas where your quest for freedom left you battered by the storms of persecution and staggered by the winds of police brutality. You have been the veterans of creative suffering. Continue to work with the faith that unearned suffering is redemptive.
>
> Go back to Mississippi. Go back to Alabama. Go back to South Carolina. Go back to Georgia. Go back to Louisiana. Go back to the slums and ghettos of our northern cities, knowing that somehow this situation can and will be changed. Let us not wallow in the valley of despair.
>
> *(This is the place in the speech where Mahalia Jackson called out to Dr. King from the audience., "Tell them about the dream, Martin." King steps away from his written speech, and under Divine Inspiration speaks extemporaneously.)*
>
> I say to you today, my friends, that in spite of the difficulties and frustrations of the moment, I still have a dream. It is a dream deeply rooted in the American dream.
>
> I have a dream that one day this nation will rise up and live out the true meaning of its creed: "We hold these truths to be self-evident: that all men are created equal."

I have a dream that one day on the red hills of Georgia the sons of former slaves and the sons of former slave owners will be able to sit down together at a table of brotherhood.

I have a dream that one day even the state of Mississippi, a state sweltering with the heat of injustice, sweltering with the heat of oppression, will be transformed into an oasis of freedom and justice.

I have a dream that my four little children will one day live in a nation where they will not be judged by the color of their skin but by the content of their character.

I have a dream today. I have a dream that one day, down in Alabama, with its vicious racists, with its governor having his lips dripping with the words of interposition and nullification; one day right there in Alabama, little black boys and black girls will be able to join hands with little white boys and white girls as sisters and brothers.

I have a dream today. I have a dream that one day every valley shall be exalted, every hill and mountain shall be made low, the rough places will be made plain, and the crooked places will be made straight, and the glory of the Lord shall be revealed, and all flesh shall see it together.

This is our hope. This is the faith with which I return to the South. With this faith, we will be able to hew out of the mountain of despair a stone of hope. With this faith, we will be able to transform the jangling discords of our nation into a beautiful symphony of brotherhood.

With this faith, we will be able to work together, to pray together, to struggle together, to go to jail together, to stand up for freedom together, knowing that we will be free one day.

This will be the day when all of God's children will be able to sing with a new meaning, "My country, 'tis of Thee, sweet land of liberty, of thee I sing. Land where my fathers died, land of the pilgrim's pride, from every mountainside, let freedom ring."

And if America is to be a great nation this must become true.

So let freedom ring from the prodigious hilltops of New Hampshire!

Let freedom ring from the mighty mountains of New York!

Let freedom ring from the heightening Alleghenies of Pennsylvania!

Let freedom ring from the snowcapped Rockies of Colorado!

Let freedom ring from the curvaceous peaks of California!

But not only that; let freedom ring from Stone Mountain of Georgia!

Let freedom ring from Lookout Mountain of Tennessee!

King's March on Washington - U.S. Government Photo

Let freedom ring from every hill and every molehill of Mississippi. From every mountainside, let freedom ring!

When we let freedom ring, when we let it ring from every village and every hamlet, from every state and every city, we will be able to speed up that day when all of God's children, black men and white men, Jews and Gentiles, Protestants and Catholics, will be able to join hands and sing in the words of the old Negro spiritual, "Free at last! Free at last! Thank God Almighty, we are free at last!"

Rhetorical Analysis of Dr. King's "I Have a Dream"

Take a look at this short rhetorical analysis of Dr. King's "I Have a Dream" speech. There are five key lessons in speech making that we can extract from the most famous portion of Dr. King's speech quoted above. Please look back at the speech and find the key elements listed below:

1. Repeat key phrases at the beginning of sentences.

"Some of you have come" - 3 successive times

"Go back to" - 6 successive times

"I have a dream" - 7 successive times

"With this faith" - 3 successive times

"Let freedom ring" - 8 successive times

2. Repeat key "theme" words throughout the speech.

a. Mountain Theme - *10 times*

Mountain of despair

Prodigious *hilltops* of New Hampshire

Mighty *mountains* of New York.

Heightening *Alleghenies* of Pennsylvania

The snowcapped *Rockies* of Colorado

Curvaceous *peaks* of California

Stone Mountain of Georgia

Lookout Mountain of Tennessee

Every *hill* and every *molehill* of Mississippi

From every *mountainside* let freedom ring

Every hill and *mountain* shall be made low

  b. Let Freedom Ring Theme - *12 times (12th time rephrased)*

From every mountainside, *let freedom ring.*"

So *let freedom ring* from the prodigious hilltops of New Hampshire.

Let freedom ring from the mighty mountains of New York.

Let freedom ring from the heightening Alleghenies of Pennsylvania!

Let freedom ring from the snowcapped Rockies of Colorado!

Let freedom ring from the curvaceous peaks of California!

But not only that; *let freedom ring* from Stone Mountain of Georgia!

Let freedom ring from Lookout Mountain of Tennessee!

Let freedom ring from every hill and every molehill of Mississippi.

From every mountainside, *let freedom ring*!

When we *let freedom ring,* when we *let it ring* from every village and every hamlet, from every state and every city

4. Use appropriate quotations or allusions. Make historic or literary references using direct quotations. (An allusion is an expression designed to call something to mind without mentioning it explicitly; an indirect or passing reference.) Dr. King uses historical and biblical allusions to back up the moral rectitude of his words and to prick what was at that time the Christian conscience of the nation.

Allusions:

a. "Let us not wallow in the valley of despair...all God's children will be able to join hands and sing."

> Allusion to Hosea 2:15, 23: "I will give her vineyards from there, and the Valley of Achor (despair) as a door of hope; She shall sing there."

b. "With this faith, we will be able to hew out of the mountain of despair a stone of hope."

> Allusion to Daniel 2:34-35, 44: from Nebuchadnezzar's dream, "A stone was cut out of the mountain without hands, which smote the image upon the feet that were of iron and clay, and broke them to pieces. . . In those days, the God of heaven will set up a kingdom, which shall never be destroyed: and the kingdom shall not be left to other people, but it shall break in pieces and consume all these kingdoms, and it shall stand for ever."

c. "I have a dream today that every valley shall be exalted, every hill and mountain shall be made low, the rough places will be made plain, and the crooked places will be made straight, and the glory of the Lord shall be revealed, and all flesh shall see it together."

> Allusion to Isaiah 40:3-5: "The voice of one crying in the wilderness:"Prepare the way of the Lord; Make straight in the desert a highway for our God. Every valley shall be exalted And every mountain and hill brought low; The

crooked places shall be made straight And the rough places smooth; The glory of the Lord shall be revealed, And all flesh shall see it together; For the mouth of the Lord has spoken."

d. "And when this happens, . . . we will be able to speed up that day when all of God's children, black men and white men, Jews and Gentiles, Protestants and Catholics, will be able to join hands and sing".

> Allusion to Galatians 3:28: "There is neither Jew nor Greek, there is neither bond nor free, there is neither male nor female: for you are all one in Christ Jesus."

e. "You have been the veterans of creative suffering. Continue to work with the faith that unearned suffering is redemptive."

> Allusion to Genesis 37-50: Joseph's suffering as a slave in Egypt brought him to the second position of rulership in Egypt and saved his family from famine. Joseph could say, "You meant evil against me, but God meant it for good."

> Allusion to 2 Corinthians 1:4-6: "God comforts us in all our troubles so that we can comfort others. When we are weighed down with troubles, it is for your comfort and salvation!"

Quotations:

a. Quote from the Declaration of Independence: "We hold these truths to be self-evident: that all men are created equal."

b. Quote from Isaiah 40:4-5: "every valley shall be exalted, every hill and mountain shall be made low, the rough places will be made plain, and the crooked places will be made straight, and the glory of the Lord shall be revealed, and all flesh shall see it together."

c. Quote from patriotic hymn *My Country 'Tis of Thee:* "My country, 'tis of Thee, sweet land of liberty, of thee I sing. Land where my fathers died, land of the pilgrim's pride, from every mountainside, let freedom ring."

d. Quote from old Negro Spiritual: "Free at last! Free at last! Thank God Almighty, we are free at last!"

4. Use specific examples to "ground" your arguments.

Dr. King refers to oppression specifically in the following places:

Georgia: Prejudice and a lack of brotherhood: "the sons of former slaves and the sons of former slave owners will be able to sit down together at a table of brotherhood."

Mississippi: "a state sweltering with the heat of injustice, sweltering with the heat of oppression".

Alabama: "with its vicious racists, with its governor".

King refers to Mississippi, Alabama, South Carolina, Louisiana and the slums and ghettos of our northern cities as places of despair. King indirectly alludes to oppression in these places where he proclaims that freedom must ring: New Hampshire, New York, Pennsylvania, Colorado, California, Tennessee

5. Use contrasting phrases and metaphors to highlight concepts: (A metaphor is a figure of speech in which a term or phrase is applied to something to which it is not literally applicable in order to suggest a resemblance, as in "A mighty fortress is our God.")

Contrasting Metaphors:

"Quest for freedom left you battered by the storms of persecution and staggered by the winds of police brutality".

"Heat of injustice, sweltering with the heat of oppression, will be transformed into an oasis of freedom and justice"

"Every valley shall be exalted, every hill and mountain shall be made low, the rough places will be made plain, and the crooked places will be made straight"

"Hew out of the mountain of despair a stone of hope"

"Transform the jangling discords of our nation into a beautiful symphony of brotherhood"

Contrasting Phrases:

"The sons of former slaves and the sons of former slave owners"

"Black boys and black girls will be able to join hands with little white boys and white girls as sisters and brothers"

Dr. King's "I Have a Dream" speech:
https://goo.gl/mTmNTo

Dr. King, "Drum Major for Righteousness"

Dr. King once declared: "Until you conquer the fear of death, you don't know what freedom is!" And what was the great idea that motivated King's bold stand for Truth and his eloquence as a speaker? We find it in his Christian testimony. A portion of the audio tape of one of his sermons was played at his funeral. The speech is entitled *Drum Major Instinct*:

If any of you are around when I have to meet my day, I don't want a long funeral. And if you get somebody to deliver the eulogy, tell them not to talk too long. Every now and then I wonder what I want them to say. Tell them not to mention that I have a Nobel Peace Prize, that isn't important. Tell them not to mention that I have three or four hundred other awards, that's not important. Tell him not to mention where I went to school.

I'd like somebody to mention that day that Martin Luther King, Jr. tried to give his life serving others. I'd like for somebody to say that day that Martin Luther King, Jr. tried to love somebody. I want you to say that day that I tried to be right on the war question. I want you to be able to say that day that I did try to feed the hungry. I want you to be able to say that day that I did try in my life to clothe those who were naked. I want you to say on that day that I did try in my life to visit those who were in prison. I want you to say that I tried to love and serve humanity.

Yes, if you want to, say that I was a drum major, say that I was a drum major for justice; say that I was a drum major for peace; I was a drum major for righteousness. And all of the other shallow things will not matter. I won't have any money to leave behind. I won't have the fine and luxurious things of life to leave behind. But I just want to leave a committed life behind.

Listen to part of Dr. King's Drum Major Instinct played at Dr. King's funeral: https://goo.gl/yVocj3

Dr. King's "Drum Major Instinct" - complete speech: https://goo.gl/nSRUiv

Dr. King's Final Speech - "I've Been to the Mountain Top" - King was assassinated the next morning: https://goo.gl/F9nev7

Ronald Reagan, U.S. President and Architect of Freedom, The Great Communicator

Consider the unforgettable oratory of Ronald Reagan as he stood in West Berlin before the Brandenburg Gate that had been closed by the Soviet Union. Separating East from West, this gate had been the site of the death of many trying to escape from slavery to communism to freedom in the West. The gate had become a part of the Berlin Wall, a twelve-foot concrete wall extending for a hundred miles, surrounding West Berlin, and included electrified fences and guard posts. This wall, built by the Soviets to keep their people from escaping into the West, stood as a stark symbol of the decades-old Cold War between the

Ronald Reagan, 40th President
Courtesy of the Ronald Reagan Library

United States and Soviet Russia in which the two politically and philosophically opposed superpowers continually wrestled for dominance, stopping just short of actual warfare. The Soviet Union's official belief system was entrenched in atheism and their belief that "religion was the opiate of the people." The state and man were believed to be their own god. It was their stated goal to bring the whole world under atheistic communism. They held Karl Marx's view of history - that communism was "the pinnacle toward which all history was moving," and were busy trying to realize this goal.

The United States, on the other hand, stood fast in her Christian belief that it was God who was the Creator and Director of the universe and the affairs of humankind. Americans believed that God had given every person inalienable rights to life, liberty, and the pursuit of happiness. This belief echoed in the heart of her school children every day as they pledged allegiance to the flag: "One nation under God, indivisible, with liberty and justice for all!" On the U.S. money written in letters large enough for all the world to read was inscribed her motto: "In God We Trust!"

When Reagan arrived at the Brandenburg Gate for the ceremonies, he had been taken to a government building to wait. His German hosts told him not to stand too close to the window because, across the wall, the East Berlin Communist government had special eavesdropping equipment so they could listen in on conversations. Reagan writes in his autobiography, "When I heard that, I went out to a landing that was even closer to the building and began sounding off about what I thought of a government that penned in its people like farm animals." [45]

Reagan later told some friends that he and his staff had an earnest disagreement over the words he wanted to say in his speech that day. His advisers warned him that saying such radical things could set back the new relationship that he was building with Michael Gorbachev, the leader of the Soviet Union. Regardless, President Reagan was determined to keep the remarks in his speech. Here is a short excerpt:

> Behind me stands a wall that encircles the free sectors of this city, part of a vast system of barriers that divides the entire continent of Europe. From the Baltic, south, those barriers cut across Germany in a gash of barbed wire, concrete, dog

**Ronald Reagan, 40th President of the United States at
Brandenburg Gate, West Berlin, Germany**

Courtesy of the Ronald Reagan Library

runs, and guard towers. Farther south, there may be no
visible, no obvious wall. But there remain armed guards and
checkpoints all the same - still a restriction on the right to
travel, still an instrument to impose upon ordinary men and
women the will of a totalitarian state. Yet, it is here in Berlin
where the wall emerges most clearly; here, cutting across
your city, where the news photo and the television screen
have imprinted this brutal division of a continent upon the
mind of the world. Standing before the Brandenburg Gate,
every man is a German, separated from his fellowmen. Every
man is a Berliner, forced to look upon a scar.

Today I say: As long as the gate is closed, as long as this scar of a wall is permitted to stand, it is not the German question alone that remains open, but the question of freedom for all mankind.

In the 1950s, Khrushchev predicted: "We will bury you." But in the West today, we see a free world that has achieved a level of prosperity and well-being unprecedented in all human history. In the Communist world, we see failure, technological backwardness, declining standards of health, even want of the most basic kind - too little food. Even today, the Soviet Union still cannot feed itself. After these four decades, then, there stands before the entire world one great and inescapable conclusion: Freedom leads to prosperity. Freedom replaces the ancient hatreds among the nations with comity and peace. Freedom is the victor.

And now the Soviets themselves may, in a limited way, be coming to understand the importance of freedom. We hear much from Moscow about a new policy of reform and openness. Some political prisoners have been released. Certain foreign news broadcasts are no longer being jammed. Some economic enterprises have been permitted to operate with greater freedom from state control.

Are these the beginnings of profound changes in the Soviet State? Or are they token gestures, intended to raise false hopes in the West, or to strengthen the Soviet system without changing it? We welcome change and openness; for we believe that freedom and security go together, that the advance of human liberty can only strengthen the cause of world peace. There is one sign the Soviets can make that would be unmistakable, that would advance dramatically the cause of freedom and peace.

General Secretary Gorbachev, if you seek peace, if you seek prosperity for the Soviet Union and Eastern Europe, if you seek liberalization: Come here to this gate! Mr. Gorbachev, open this gate! Mr. Gorbachev, tear down this wall!

On November 4, 1989, the East German government, a satellite of the Soviet Union, announced that the Brandenburg Gate and all border crossings were open for people to come and go freely. Recalling the event, Reagan writes, "Standing so near the Berlin Wall, seeing it in substance as well as for what it symbolized, I felt an anger well up in me and I am sure this anger was reflected in my voice when I said those words. I never dreamed that in less than three years the wall would come down and a six-thousand-pound section of it would be sent to me for my presidential library."[46]

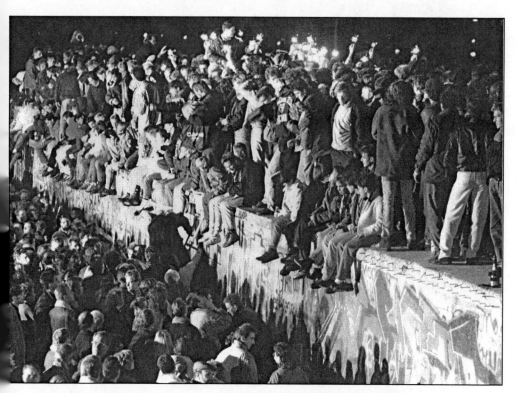

The Berlin Wall was Torn Down by the German People, November 9, 1989

© European Press photo Agency - used by permission

Video of President Reagan's "Berlin Wall"Speech at Brandenburg Gate, from the Ronald Reagan library:
https://goo.gl/hXa8bh

Watch the Dramatic Video of the Berlin Wall Coming Down
https://goo.gl/P4d5Vr

The History of the Wall - So We Will Never Forget What Communism is About: https://goo.gl/5dpPKY
https://goo.gl/aqqt1E

Reagan, On Religious Freedom

Prime Minister Gorbachev and President Reagan In Friendship Let Freedom Ring!

Courtesy of Ronald Reagan Library

What of Reagan's faith? When he was invited for a visit to Russia, Reagan writes that he took this opportunity to bring up a subject that had been on his mind for a long time - religious freedom. Speaking to Prime Minister Gorbachev, Reagan said, "Our country was started by people who were not allowed to worship as they wished in their homeland, so they came to our shores, a wilderness across the Atlantic, and founded our Nation. I'm sure a lot of your people who are asking to leave wouldn't want to leave if they had freedom of religion. I know they must love their country ... if you allowed them to worship as they want to, they might decide that they wouldn't have to leave."

Reflecting on this conversation, Reagan writes, "Whether my words had any impact or not I don't know, but after that the Soviet government began allowing more churches and synagogues to reopen, and of course, in time the wall came tumbling down." [47]

What does this tell us? It shows us the power of words rightly spoken to move and change the hearts of men. Destinies of nations hang in the balance and have been changed through the power of words. This proves what Jesus told over 2,000 years ago, "You will know the truth, and the truth will set you free." Maybe that is why Jesus told His disciples to go everywhere and preach the truth regardless of the personal cost. "What you hear whispered in the ear," He told His disciples, "shout from the housetops!"

What was the great motivating idea behind Reagan's oratory? He explains, "For more than thirty years I had been preaching about freedom and liberty and against communism." [48]

Reagan, Visit to Moscow State University

Reagan recounts that during his visit, Gorbachev invited him to speak at Moscow State University to some of the brightest minds in the Soviet Union - something he had never dreamed would be possible. He felt that this was his chance to speak to the future leaders of the Soviet Union about the blessings of liberty. It was an opportunity to change things. Here is a short excerpt:

> It's hard for government planners, no matter how sophisticated to ever substitute for millions of individuals working night and day to make their dreams come true ...
> We Americans make no secret of our belief in freedom ...
> Freedom is the right to put forth an idea, scoffed at by the

experts, and watch it catch fire among the people. It is the right to dream - to follow your dream or stick to your conscience, even if you're the only one in a sea of doubters.

Freedom is the recognition that no single person, no single authority or government has a monopoly on the truth, but that every individual life is infinitely precious, that every one of us put on this world has been put there for a reason and has something to offer ...

Your generation is living in one of the most exciting, hopeful times in Soviet history. It is a time when the first breath of freedom stirs the air and the heart beats to the accelerated rhythm of hope, when the accumulated spiritual energies of a long silence yearn to break free.

I am reminded of the famous passage near the end of Gogol's *Dead Souls*. Comparing his nation to a speeding troika, Gogol asks what will be its destination. But he writes, "There was no answer save the bell pouring forth marvelous sound."

We may be allowed to hope that the marvelous sound of a new openness will keep rising through, ringing through, leading to a new world of reconciliation, friendship and peace.

Listen President Reagan's "Speech at Moscow State University" courtesy of the Reagan Library:
https://goo.gl/i8umRW

Reagan, The Result of His Oratory

And what happened in the Soviet Union primarily as a result of Reagan's determination to preach at every opportunity on the blessings of freedom and liberty and against the diabolical oppression of socialism and communism? Things changed everywhere. All the nations in the Eastern Block that had been annexed to the Soviet Union against their will broke free and became independent. The doors to civil, economic, and religious freedom swung wide open. In the atmosphere of new-found religious freedom, God poured out His Spirit, and multitudes of Russians and people from former satellite states of the Soviet Union were swept into the kingdom of God in a genuine spiritual awakening. The leaders of Russia became friendly with the church and rewrote their national constitution to include religious, civil, and economic freedom.

In April of 2009, Russian Prime Minister Putin spoke to an economic summit in Switzerland and warned the West of the dangers of sliding into socialism/Marxism:

> During the time of the Soviet Union, the role of the state in the economy was made absolute, which eventually led to the total non-competitiveness of the economy. That lesson cost us very dearly. I am sure nobody would want history to repeat itself. We should also be aware that during the last months, we have been witnessing the washout of the entrepreneurship spirit *in the West*. That includes the principle of personal responsibility – of a businessman, an investor, or a share-holder – for his or her own decisions. There are no grounds to suggest that by putting the responsibility over to the state, one can achieve better results.[49]

What does this tell us? Marxism is doomed to failure. Marx once proclaimed that Communism was the pinnacle toward which all history is moving. Among other things, Communism is a system where all responsibility is on the state to provide for its citizens and everything is held in common. The state is god, atheism is the belief, and people do not have a right to hold an individual opinion that contradicts the state mantra. A person must be politically correct.

President Reagan predicted this in 1982, nine years before the collapse of the Soviet Union and their Marxist government. He said:

> It is the Soviet Union that runs against the tide of history ... It is the march of freedom and democracy which will leave Marxism-Leninism on the ash heap of history as it has left other tyrannies which stifle the freedom and muzzle the self-expression of the people.[30]

Russia has decided that it is not only moral economics but good economics to encourage their people to take personal responsibility for their own lives - the state will no longer do it for them. Freedom to invest, freedom to own their own businesses and their own homes, freedom to keep and enjoy the fruit of their labor has made all hands industrious and has plummeted the Russian people into unprecedented prosperity.

At the time of the writing of this book, Russia is advising Europe on how to get out of their economic woes. I think the advice might be - "Ditch your socialist ideas, drop the crippling regulations on your businesses and embrace freedom - freedom works!" - I wonder where they first heard that?

Who would have ever thought that words could have accomplished so much? Charles Coffin, nineteenth-century historian explains it this way:

> I have spoken of the meaning of history. Surely history has a meaning, or what are we living for. All the motives by which men are actuated - passions, affections, religious convictions, the selfish ends - are part of the grand drama of Time. Men die, generations come and go, but ideas live on. Tyranny and wrong have fought against Liberty and Justice - but Tyranny and Wrong have gone down before it. Through all

the narratives of wars, massacres, and bloodshed you will see Right, Justice, and Liberty ever advancing. Whoever fails to recognize this feature will fail to understand history's meaning.[51]

Commenting on the legendary power of his rhetoric and oratory skills, President Reagan had this to say:

> I won a nickname, "The Great Communicator." But I never thought it was my style or the words I used that made a difference: it was the content. I wasn't a great communicator, but I communicated great things, and they didn't spring full blown from my brow, they came from the heart of a great nation - from our experience, our wisdom, and our belief in the principles that have guided us for two centuries.[52]

In 1961, the Soviets built the Berlin Wall. During those years, on the evening news, clips were shown of the work the East Germans and the Soviets were doing to lengthen and strengthen the wall to keep their people from escaping. For those who watched the broadcasts during that era, the dramatic difference between belief in God and atheism, between freedom and slavery were driven home.

Clips were shown of East German citizens trying to escape being shot and killed by soldiers who guarded the wall. This wall was also known as the "Iron Curtain." In a televised speech in 1964 supporting the candidacy of Barry Goldwater for President, Reagan shares the message that was the foundation of all of his oratory. Here are a few of Reagan's remarks about the "Iron Curtain" from his speech *A Time for Choosing*. This is the speech that launched Reagan's political career.

> We cannot buy our security, our freedom from the threat of the bomb by committing an immorality so great as saying to

a billion now in slavery behind the Iron Curtain, "Give up your dreams of freedom because to save our own skin, we are willing to make a deal with your slave masters."

Should Moses have told the children of Israel to live in slavery under the pharaohs? Should Christ have refused the cross? Should the patriots at Concord Bridge have thrown down their guns and refused to fire the shot heard "round the world"?

The martyrs of history were not fools, and our honored dead who gave their lives to stop the advance of the Nazis didn't die in vain. Where, then, is the road to peace? Well, it's a simple answer after all. You and I have a rendezvous with destiny. We will preserve for our children this, the last best hope of man on Earth, or we will sentence them to take the last step into a thousand years of darkness.

On July 4, 2011, a statue commemorating what would have been Ronald Reagan's 100 birthday was unveiled in London. William Hague, Secretary of State for the British Foreign Ministry had this to say:

Statues bring us face to face with our heroes long after they are gone. Ronald Reagan is without question a great American hero; one of America's finest sons, and a giant of 20th Century history.

What a man! What a message!

Watch Reagan's "A Time for Choosing" a televised campaign address for the Barry Goldwater Presidential Campaign: https://goo.gl/jXagMV

Watch the Unveiling and Dedication Speech of Statue to Ronald Reagan in London by William Hague Secretary of State for British Foreign Ministry, July 4, 2011:https://goo.gl/LXFizU

Five

How to Get Over Stage Fright
One Young Man's Discovery

Slowly, a young man made his way across the beautiful grounds of Dartmouth College. The campus was shaded by crimson trees that were proudly displaying the colors of fall. Lost in thought, this young man was remembering the events that brought him to this hour. It was the early days of the young American Republic; the war for Independence had been won the year before he was born. He could count his age by the event. He remembered when his dad had gone to a meeting to vote to ratify the Constitution of the United States of America.

"What is the Constitution, Father?" he had asked. His dad explained the importance of the Constitution and the meaning of *union*. "If we don't hang together, we'll hang separately," his father said. He meant that unless the states stood together, they would surely become an easy target for the British. Everyone knew of the possibility that the British would come back to the Eastern seaboard and try to again take over the colonies who had recently won their independence.

If they British took back America, they would all be punished one by one. For those who had fought for American Independence that meant certain death - certain death for his father and members of his family. His dad had fought in that war along with many of their other relatives and close friends. So it was very important to make sure that the colonies joined together to form a government.

He remembered the day when his dad came home from that meeting and the family had all rushed to meet him at the door. "What happened?" they all asked. "It's all right!" his dad exclaimed. "New Hampshire voted for the Constitution. We're a nation now - the United States of America!" His dad waved his hat over his head and shouted, "Hurrah!" and all the family had joined in, "Hurrah, hurrah for the United States of America!" Then his dad said, "May God bless the Union!" These were words that he would never forget as long as he lived.

New Hampshire was the ninth state and the final one that was needed to ratify the Constitution before it could become law. How he wished he had been old enough to have been at that meeting. Since that day, he had been interested in the Constitution and the new government. He remembered the daily newspapers that arrived at his home. He learned to read in a one-room school house so he had the privilege of reading the newspapers to his family. He loved reading every bit of news about the new Republic. He had also been taught to read the Bible. He had memorized a lot of it by heart.

He loved the Good Book. What a privilege to read a book that so many saints had laid their lives down to publish. He knew there were things written in the Bible that kings and rulers didn't want people to know about. He knew the Bible's main theme was that Jesus Christ came to save the world and set people free. Wasn't the rallying cry of the Revolution, "We will have no King but Jesus!" Yes, it was, and so it is - and by God's grace so ever shall it be.

He knew the Founders of America came here for religious freedom so they could read the Bible and worship God according to the direction of their own hearts. That is the reason they made sure the right to freedom of religion, speech, press, and petition were protected in the Constitution. In the Bill of Rights, the First Amendment to the Constitution stated: "Congress shall make no law respecting an establishment of religion, or prohibiting the free exercise thereof; or abridging the freedom of speech, or of the press; or the right of the people peaceably to assemble, and to petition the Government for a redress of grievances." He knew what it said - he had memorized it long ago.

Once his dad was selected to be a judge in a robbery case. There was the main judge and then two side judges selected from among the citizens. His dad was one of these. Oh, how he begged his dad to let him go with him to court. Without hesitating his dad said yes. It was that day in court that he first started thinking about being a lawyer when he grew up. At first, he hadn't been positive whether he wanted to be a person of books or to be a farmer and work the land like the rest of his family. But there was something about his love for the law and books that pulled on him.

One day when his dad asked had him what he wanted to be when he grew up, he said unhesitatingly, "I want to be a Congressman." It just popped out of his mouth without even thinking about it. His father answered, "The Lord willing, so you shall!" The young man mused, "I guess on that day it had been settled."

He remembered the day he went to the store for his mother. As he was leaving to go back home, he saw a beautiful handkerchief spread out on the counter with writing all over it. He had never seen anything like it before. Books were scarce in those days so when he saw anything with words on it, he would always read it. The words on the handkerchief said, "The Constitution of the United States." This was what his father had told him about.

He believed if he was gong to be a lawyer and a Congressman, he had to study that Constitution. The lady running the store told him it cost twenty-six cents. He ran home to try to think of a way to get the money. He had eleven cents, but he still needed fourteen cents more. It was then he remembered a knife he won in school. His brother really liked that knife. "Maybe he will buy it from me," he had thought.

It was his good fortune that his brother said, "Yes, I will give you eighteen cents for it." With his eleven cents, he had more than enough money. He ran back to the store and bought the handkerchief. On his way home, he sat down beside the road to read it. "We the people of the United States, in order to form a more perfect union," it said. "The Union," he thought, "yes, Dad had said, 'May God bless the Union!'" He knew what this phrase meant. He decided this called for a speech. Quickly making sure no one was in sight, he climbed up on a stump. "Gentleman of Congress, I wish to speak to you about the Union. We have formed this Union to have liberty and justice for all."

How he loved the Constitution that was printed on that handkerchief. He read it over and over again until he learned it by heart. How his heart had trilled at these words. He thought about the words all the time and pondered their meaning. He knew that in order to be a Congressman, he had to learn how to give speeches. On the farm he had no place to practice giving speeches to people, so he went to the fields and made up speeches and practiced speaking to the cows and the sheep.

Well, the day finally came when his father had saved enough money to send him to school. He had no formal schooling to speak of. He would never forget how he felt when he left home. It had been a hard thing to do to say goodbye to his brother and sister. And wouldn't you know it - the first thing the teacher asked him to do when he got to school was to give a speech on Friday. He remembered how he had gone back into his room, taken out the handkerchief with the Constitution on it, and started to work out a speech about it in his head from memory. "This will be a grand speech," he thought.

Friday morning came, and when his name was called, he began to feel sick with fright. He stood up, but his legs were weak, and he was afraid he would fall down. He walked slowly to the platform and stubbed his toe. He almost fell flat, but he caught himself just in time. As he looked up and saw the audience, his face turned white; he opened his mouth, but no words came out. He couldn't remember a single thing he had planned to say. He quickly went back to his seat and sat down. He had felt like a complete failure.

In spite of this, he had studied hard and moved ahead faster than any of the boys in school. But, no matter how hard he tried, he couldn't make a speech. One day his father arrived to take him home because the family had no more money to spare for his education. "I didn't want to be a lawyer that much anyway," he told his dad. "Don't give up on your dream, son. We will get the money yet," was his father's reply. Although he was still very young, the community knew he was a good reader and begged him to teach the children there to read. He took the job as a teacher, even though he felt that he was not old enough, and to his amazement everything had gone well.

One night, his family was holding a Christmas party. After all the festivities, his uncle had asked him in front of all the family to make a speech. He felt that same sick feeling again. His face began to turn white. Then he remembered that he was a good reader. He would read everyone his favorite poem.

After he finished, no one spoke for a while, reflecting on the things he had read. "That was mighty fine," his uncle told him. But that poem and those words hadn't been his own words. "How will I ever be able to make a speech?" he had thought. Everyone knew that if you couldn't make a speech, you could never be a Congressman. His dream seemed further away than ever.

It wasn't long before his dad had been able to get together some more money. This time, his father sent him to Dartmouth College to study law. And now, here he was. He was studying hard at college and was doing well, but one thing worried him still. He knew that they would most likely call on him to make a speech any day now. What would he do? What would he say?

The young man emerged from his memories as he made his way into class, found his seat, and opened his book about Roman history. Today, as the class was discussing the text, one of the students chimed in, "I wish we had a government more like Rome. Our constitution is a failure." Another student added, "Yes, if we have any trouble, it will fall apart."

When the students made these remarks everything within him wanted to resist what they were saying. He wasn't sure exactly what was happening to him, but he felt himself trembling inside. He thought about the handkerchief and how much he loved the words that were printed on it. Suddenly, he could take it no more. He jumped to his feet and shouted:

No, it's not right. I challenge anyone to find a better plan of government than our Constitution. Anywhere in the world - now or in the past. When did abler men ever come together to make a nation? What statesmen were greater or wiser than Madison or Washington? Where did as many as thirteen separate states ever before form themselves into a Union?

There is no nobler piece of writing than our Constitution. Rome had nothing to equal it. Britain has nothing. Greece had nothing. Ours is a nation made by the will of the people. And look for what noble purposes it was established - to form a more perfect Union, establish justice, promote the general welfare, and secure the blessings of liberty! Do you know every word of it as I do? No, for if you did, you would love it and praise it as I do!

He sat down, but his eyes were still flashing. The room was very quiet. "A very fine speech, my boy," said the teacher. [53]

A speech! He had made a speech; he didn't even have a chance to rehearse it. He had no idea what he would say when he stood up. He just knew he had to defend the Constitution. All his knowledge, all his love of the Constitution came pouring out of his heart at that moment. The young man's name was Daniel Webster.

That day Daniel Webster found that the promise Jesus made to His disciples long ago was still true, "When you are called to give an account, do not worry about how or what you should answer. For the Holy Spirit will teach you at that hour what you are to say ... But the Helper, the Holy Spirit, whom the Father will send in My name, He will teach you all things, and bring to your remembrance all things that I said to you." (Luke 12:11-12; John 14:26)

Daniel Webster, Orator and Statesman - His Secret

After that, Daniel Webster was never afraid to make a speech again. He had learned two great secrets. First, when your heart is on fire with a message, it is easy to burst into a speech at a moment's notice. Second, as you step out in faith to speak up for Truth, you can trust the Holy Spirit, the Helper, to give you the words to say and bring the things He has taught you to your remembrance. One of the great promises of the New Covenant is "they shall all be taught by God." (John 6:45) If you will take time to tune in to the Holy Spirit and pray that "the words of your mouth and the meditations of your heart will be acceptable in God's sight" and ask God to infuse you with his thoughts, your inspirations and ideas will come to be God-breathed, whatever the subject. (Ps.19)

Daniel Webster went on to become one of America's greatest statesmen, and according to historians, Webster was

Daniel Webster - "Black Dan"
(1782-1852) *by Francis Alexander*

America's most pre-eminent orator - "an orator like no other." [54] His speeches have been studied and analyzed by scholars down through the years.

It was Daniel Webster's speeches in Congress that helped cement the Union. He helped people learn and understand the greatness of our nation and its founding document. People came to Congress to hear Daniel Webster speak. His speeches were printed in newspapers all over the country, and many people memorized them by heart.

Daniel Webster, His Faith

And what of Webster's faith? Was he just a good speech writer, or was it something more? In his speech to the New York National Historical Society on *The Dignity and Importance of History*, Webster ends his speech with this:

> Unborn ages and visions of glory crowd upon my soul, the realization of which, however, is in the hands and good pleasure of Almighty God, but, under His divine blessing, it will be dependent on the character and the virtues of ourselves and our posterity ...

If we and our posterity shall be true to the Christian religion, if we and they shall live always in the fear of God, and shall respect His commandments, if we and they shall maintain just moral sentiments and such conscientious convictions of duty as shall control the heart and life, we may have the highest hopes of the future fortunes of our country.

If we maintain those institutions of government and that political union, it will exceed all praise as much as it exceeds all former examples of political associations. We may be sure of one thing, it will have no decline and fall. It will go on prospering and to prosper.

But if we and our posterity reject religious institutions and authority, violate the rules of eternal justice, trifle with the injunctions of morality, and recklessly destroy the political constitution which holds us together, no man can tell how sudden a catastrophe may overwhelm us that shall bury all our glory in profound obscurity. Should that catastrophe happen, let it have no history! Let the horrible narrative never be written!

Mr. Tappan, a contemporary of Webster's father, tells us his view of the secret of Daniel Webster's powerful oratory. Tappan said, "I don't know anyone else who can talk like him. But it isn't just talk. He feels it. That's why he can talk that way. He feels it deep inside. That is the difference between people who are just good speakers and Daniel Webster." You could say about Daniel Webster that he was a boy who had his prayers answered.

Re-enactment of Daniel Webster's speech, Plymouth Oration, December 22, 1820: https://goo.gl/NDyic8

Six

Called to Deliver a Message

One of the greatest orators of the nineteenth-century was England's Catherine Booth. She and her husband William were founders of the Salvation Army. The Salvation Army

Catherine Booth - 1829-1890
Co-Founder of the Salvation Army

movement was the spiritual revival movement of that day. In the middle of the nineteenth-century, there were more people worshiping with the Salvation Army in England than in all other churches in England combined. Catherine began her public speaking in 1860. At this time, there was a prejudice against women. It was considered a disgrace for women to speak publicly, and so among polite society, it just wasn't done. The most crucial and direct letter from Catherine to her husband William on the subject of women in ministry is dated April 9, 1855, just before their marriage in June:

> Oh I believe that volumes of light will yet be shed on the world on this subject; it will *bear examination* and abundantly repay it ... I believe woman is destined to assume her true position, and exert her proper influence by the special

exertions and attainments of her own sex ... May the Lord, even the just and Impartial One, overrule all for the true emancipation of women from swaddling bands of prejudice, ignorance, and custom, which almost the world over have so long debased and wronged her. [55]

One day Catherine Booth was feeling very dark and depressed as she was sitting in the church meeting with her eldest son. She writes about her first experience with public speaking:

As the testimonies proceeded, I felt the Holy Spirit come upon me. It seemed as if a Voice said to me: "Now, if you were to go and testify, you know I would bless it to your own soul as well as to the people!" I gasped again, and said in my heart: "Yes, Lord, I believe You would, but I cannot do it!"

A moment afterwards there flashed across my mind the memory of the time when I had promised the Lord that I would obey Him at all costs. And then the Voice seemed to ask me if this was consistent with that promise. I almost jumped up and said, "No, Lord, it is the old thing over again. But I cannot do it!" I felt as though I would sooner die than speak. And then the Devil said, "Besides, you are not prepared. You will look like a fool, and will have nothing to say." He made a mistake. He overreached himself for once. It was this word that settled it. "Ah!" I said, "This is just the point. I have never yet been willing to be a fool for Christ. Now I will be one!"

Without stopping another moment, I rose up from my seat and walked down the aisle. My dear husband thought something had happened to me, and so did the people. We had been there two years, and they knew my timid, bashful nature. He stepped down, and asked me, "What is the matter, my dear?" I replied, "I want to say a word!" He was so taken by surprise that he could only say, "My dear wife wishes to speak!" and sat down. For years he had been trying to persuade me to do it. Only that very week he had wanted me to go and address a little Cottage Meeting of some twenty working people, but I had refused.

I stood - God only knows how - and if any mortal ever did hang on the arm of Omnipotence, I did. I just stood and told the people how it had come about. I confessed, as I think everybody should who has been in the wrong and has misrepresented the religion of Jesus Christ. I said, "I dare say many of you have been looking upon me as a very devoted woman, and one who has been living faithfully to God. But I have come to realize that I have been disobeying Him, and thus brought darkness and leanness into my soul. I have promised the Lord to do so no longer, and have come to tell you that henceforth I will be obedient to the holy vision.

There was more weeping, they said, in the chapel that day than on any previous occasion. Many dated a renewal in righteousness from that very moment, and began a life of devotion and consecration to God.[56]

Catherine Booth, Orator and Social Reformer

Catherine became one of the best-loved orators in England. On the qualifications of women to speak publicly, Catherine wrote, "God has given to woman a graceful form and attitude, winning manners, persuasive speech, and, above all, a finely-toned emotional nature, all of which appear to us eminent natural qualifications for public speaking."[57] Catherine Booth worked tirelessly for the spiritual conversion of England and for moral and social reformation.

One of her fights was to protect children from being used legally in prostitution. Here is a short excerpt from her speech against laws in England that made child prostitution at the age of ten legal and regulated by Parliament:

> It is my prayer that God will enable Parliament presently to blot off from the Statute Book laws so infamous. Apart from this rectifying action on the part of the Government, I must confess that the deepest feeling of my soul in rising to speak on this subject is that of intense shame! Shame that it should be necessary at this period of our national history, to stand on this Exeter Hall platform to plead for the repeal of such measures as those you have discussed tonight.
>
> I can only conceive of one greater shame possible, and that would be, to shrink from the necessity which has been imposed upon us. I would say—Let every man and woman whose eyes are open to the tendency of these Acts remember that the genius, the spirit of these Acts, that which formed them and carried them will not rest here. The same demon which would level all distinctions between vice and virtue, morality and licentiousness, has got his eye on your religious liberties!! Look out! We have need to remember that "the price of liberty is eternal vigilance"...
>
> The same rulers who patronize vice - the same rulers who barter over the souls and bodies of unsuspecting children, pass police regulations to put down and root out all manifestations of vital godliness wherever they find it, and many of them are now engaged in the Herod-like work, hunting for the God Child in order to destroy Him. They aim at the destruction of your religious liberties, and it behoves every Christian man in this country -   lay or

ministerial - every man or woman as far as his or her ability will allow, to mount the walls of Zion, and sound down the sleeping ranks of the professed soldiers of the Cross the alarm note that they should be up and watching that this fiend should not take away liberties for which our forefathers fought and bled ...

One word more in conclusion. How are we to fight this evil? You must work, work - and I would say with reference to this movement, as I do with the one with which I am more intimately connected - if you want to help us in the great strife against evil, in the hand to hand fight with the devil - spread information - scatter intelligence - be at the trouble to open the eyes of your neighbors and friends. Give your friends pamphlets and books ...

Then, I say again, work, work, and spread information! Don't think you will repeal these Acts by wishing them repealed. Don't imagine you will repeal them by sentimentalizing about them. Nor even by praying about them, unless you work too. It is one of the greatest mistakes that people pray their hypocritical prayers, and then sit down and do nothing.

 We of the Salvation Army believe in prayer - we spend whole nights at it often - but we believe in work too. We believe God has conditioned His working on our working, and if we will use the power and influence, and talent, and spirit which God has given us, He will work with us, and God and man will combine to blot out these infamous laws for ever! [58]

After the conclusion of this message in Exeter Hall in London, a gentleman in attendance exclaimed, "If ever I am charged with a crime, don't bother to engage any of the great lawyers to defend me; get that woman!" [59] People took up the cause and these unjust laws to regulate vice were finally repealed and protection was extended under the law to children against sex trafficking in nineteenth-century England. Besides bringing untold thousands of people to a saving knowledge of Jesus Christ, Catherine's work helped change working conditions for the poor, the low wages of women, and end the practice of child labor.

Margaret Thatcher, Prime Minister of Great Britain

Margaret Thatcher, former Prime Minister of Great Britain, is among the famous orators of the twentieth century. Together with President Ronald Reagan, she worked tirelessly against the oppression of the Soviet Union and worked to rescue Britain from the depression of socialism by deregulating industry and moving it from the public sector to the private sector and transformed the economy to free enterprise economics. She privatized government-held companies and launched an era of unprecedented prosperity for the British people. Here is an excerpt from one of her famous speeches to the College of Europe, *The Bruges Speech*, in which she refers to the role Christianity has played in the development of Liberty. She begins by honoring the anniversary of the day that Prince William of Orange,

Prime Minister Margaret Thatcher
Courtesy of the Margaret Thatcher Foundation

defender of the Protestant Reformation, took the throne of England:

> This year, we celebrate the three-hundredth anniversary of the glorious revolution in which the British Crown passed to Prince William of Orange and Queen Mary. Visit the great churches and cathedrals of Britain, read our literature and listen to our language: all bear witness to the cultural riches which we have drawn from Europe and other Europeans from us. We in Britain are rightly proud of the way in which, since Magna Carta in the year 1215, we have pioneered and developed representative institutions to stand as bastions of freedom. And proud, too, of the way in which for centuries Britain was a home for people from the rest of Europe who sought sanctuary from tyranny ...
>
> From classical and medieval thought, we have borrowed that concept of the rule of law which marks out a civilized society from barbarism. And on that idea of Christendom - Christendom for long synonymous with Europe - with its recognition of the unique and spiritual nature of the individual, on that idea, we still base our belief in personal liberty and other human rights.
>
> Too often, the history of Europe is described as a series of interminable wars and quarrels. Yet, from our perspective today, surely what strikes us most is our common experience. For instance, the story of how Europeans explored and colonized - and yes, without apology - civilized much of the world is an extraordinary tale of talent, skill and courage. But, we British have in a very special way contributed to Europe.
>
> Over the centuries, we have fought to prevent Europe from falling under the dominance of a single power. We have

fought and we have died for her freedom. Only miles from here, in Belgium, lie the bodies of 120,000 British soldiers who died in the First World War. Had it not been for that willingness to fight and to die, Europe would have been united long before now — but not in liberty, not in justice. It was British support to resistance movements throughout the last War that helped to keep alive the flame of liberty in so many countries until the day of liberation. And it was from our island fortress that the liberation of Europe itself was mounted (World War II and the opposition to the Nazi occupation of Europe).

And still, today, we stand together. Nearly 70,000 British servicemen are stationed on the mainland of Europe. All these things alone are proof of our commitment to Europe's future. The European Community is *one* manifestation of that European identity, but it is not the only one. We must never forget that east of the Iron Curtain, people, who once enjoyed a full share of European culture, freedom, and identity, have been cut off from their roots ... Nor should we forget that European values have helped to make the United States of America into the valiant defender of freedom which she has become ...

Indeed, it is ironic that just when those countries such as the Soviet Union, which have tried to run everything from the center, are learning that success depends on dispersing power and decisions away from the center, there are some in the Community who seem to want to move in the opposite direction ... If Europe is to flourish and create the jobs of the future, enterprise is the key ... Our aim should *not* be more and more detailed regulation from the centre: it should be to deregulate and to remove the constraints on trade.

The Power of Margaret Thatcher's Oratory

Prime Minister Thatcher worked tirelessly to bring an end to Communism in the Soviet Union. She spoke on every occasion she could and everywhere she could on the failure of Communism and the right of the people held under its power to be free. Mrs. Thatcher teamed up with President Ronald Reagan to try to make the defeat of Communism in the Soviet Union a reality.

Mrs. Thatcher took a special interest in Poland because of the Solidarity movement which was pushing back against the Communist regime. She set up a State visit to talk with the Polish Communist leaders about setting their people free. When she arrived in Poland, she was invited to visit one of the churches. She writes in her autobiography that the church was thronged with multitudes of families. As she entered the cathedral, the whole church stood and broke out into Poland's Solidarity song, "God give us back our free Poland." When she heard their song, tears welled up in her eyes.

Unknown to her, the Polish people had been listening on the radio to her speeches demanding freedom in the Soviet Union and for the nations in Eastern Europe under Soviet domination. In reflecting on this experience in a documentary on her life, Mrs. Thatcher said the Polish people told her that her voice had been to them the voice of freedom. They said her speeches had given them great hope and convinced them that one day they would be free from the grip of Communism.

Mrs. Thatcher writes that she shook hundreds of hands in the church that day and gave a short, emotional speech. As she left, the streets were filled with people crying with emotion and shouting, "Thank you! Thank You!"   Such is the power of great oratory.

From that experience Margaret Thatcher returned to Warsaw with more determination than ever to fight to free these people from Communism. And it was not long before that day of freedom came for the Polish people. One year after Prime Minister Thatcher's visit in 1988, the Polish people were allowed to hold free elections. The Solidarity liberty forces won 99 of the 100 seats in that election, resulting in a political earthquake. They voted to set up a non-communist government. In 1989, the Polish nation withdrew from the Soviet Union and eliminated all Marxists references to the name of their country, becoming the Polish Republic once again. Amazingly they had no resistance for their decision from the Soviet Union.[60]

Thatcher, a Tribute to Ronald Reagan, a Eulogy

Here is another example of Margaret Thatcher's inspired oratory - an excerpt from her speech, *A Tribute to Ronald Reagan*, which she delivered at President Reagan's funeral. She had this to say about the fight for liberty in the world today and what made Reagan's rhetoric so compelling:

> Ronnie and I got to know each other at a time when we were both in opposition, and when a good many people intended to keep us there. They failed, and the conservative 1980s were the result.

> But in a certain sense, we remained an opposition, we were never the establishment. We were opposed to big government, to fashionable opinion within the belt-way, and to the endless round of so-called liberal solutions to problems the liberals themselves had created.

> As Ron once put it: the nine most dangerous words in the English language are "I'm from the government, and I'm here to help." As usual, he was right ... He believed, and he never stopped proclaiming, that the talents of a nation, not the wisdom of bureaucracy, forge a country's greatness. Let

our children grow tall – he urged – then they can reach out to raise others higher too.

For our opponents, there are always a hundred reasons why the government must intervene to plan its children's lives. For us, there's one overwhelming reason why it shouldn't – because men and women are born to be free. But yesterday's conservatives never imagined that the end of the Soviet Union would usher in an end to danger – only the liberals, wrong now as in the past, thought that. Those liberals were all too influential.

The West cut back its defenses too far. It weakened its intelligence effort. It succumbed to the fatal illusion that government's role is to make us comfortable, rather than to keep us safe. And so it was that those who hate America, fear liberty and attack progress, were able to prepare their wicked assault on this nation that fateful Tuesday last September 11.

I am pleased and proud that Britain, once again, has made an important contribution to this struggle against evil. Echoing both Bismarck and Churchill, President Reagan once remarked: "Future historians will note that a supreme fact of this twentieth-century was that Great Britain and the United States shared the same cause: the cause of human freedom.

My friends: in the continuation of the War Against Terror our countries must again stand firm. President Reagan didn't just abhor communism, mistrust socialism and dislike bureaucracy, he truly loved liberty – he loved it with a passion which went far beyond anything else in his political life. It was what brought moral grandeur to his vision of America and to his dreams for a better world. It was directed not mainly at earthly powers and principalities but rather at the infinitely precious, utterly unique human being, wherever he or she was yearning to breathe free. The thought is memorably expressed by the poet Byron:

> Eternal Spirit of the chain-less mind!
> Brightest in Dungeons, Liberty! Thou art,
> For there thy habitation is the heart –
> The heart which love of thee alone can bind;
>
> And when thy sons to fetters are consigned –
> To fetters, and the damp vault's day-less gloom,
> Their country conquers with their martyrdom,
> And Freedom's fame finds wings on every wind.

**Prime Minister Margaret Thatcher and
President Ronald Reagan at Camp David**

Courtesy of the Ronald Reagan Library

Watch Margaret Thatcher's Speech, "Tribute to Ronald Reagan": https://goo.gl/JDvxJU

Watch Margaret Thatcher "Last Stand Against Socialism" on the Floor of Parliament: https://goo.gl/sqB9ds

Watch Margaret Thatcher Deliver Her Famous "Bruges Speech" given in 1988 rejecting centralization of Europe: https://goo.gl/T5UJdh

Watch Margaret Thatcher Deliver Her Speech "There is No such Thing as Public Money" : https://goo.gl/WT3Fdu

The Source of Inspiration

Of all the notable people we have considered, there is one thing all of them had in common that made them master communicators and enabled them to speak such ennobling and immortal words that influenced their generation, as well as those after them. Their hearts were on fire with a message. They each had an idea and a message which they believed was important, a message which they believed came from God. Their lives were absorbed with that idea; their emotions and convictions were wrapped up in it. And because of this, they stood out from the crowd. As the Psalmist wrote thousands of years ago when his heart was bursting from within, "My heart is overflowing with a good theme; I recite my composition concerning the King; My tongue is the pen of a ready writer." (Ps. 45:1)

A.W. Tozer, often called a twentieth-century prophet, reflected on his tendency to burst into speech when his heart was full and overflowing. He wrote, "At the risk of getting myself into doubtful company, I might claim for myself the testimony of Elihu, the son of Barachel, the Buzite of the kindred of Ram from the book of Job: 'For I am full of words, and the spirit within me compels me.' I know what he means." [61]

As we have seen, the real challenge to becoming a good speaker is not trying to get over stage fright or trying to overcome that weak-in-the-knees feeling. The real challenge is to dedicate yourself to your theme until you are so sure of your message that it possesses you and compels you to speak. When someone is aflame with a message, the desire to plunge into a speech is at its maximum.

After all is said and done, you will become a great communicator when you have great ideas and thoughts to communicate. The power and inspiration of great ideas and the work of God's Spirit to back up Truth are what gave strength and courage to Peter, Stephen, and alla of Jesus' disciples, John Huss, Martin Luther, Patrick Henry, Thomas Jefferson, John Adams, George Whitefield, Daniel Webster, Abraham Lincoln, Elizabeth Cady Stanton, Dr. Martin Luther King, Ronald Reagan, Catherine Booth, and Margaret Thatcher.

Dr. King reminded us of this in the last speech he gave before his assassination, *I've been to the Mountaintop,*: "Somehow the preacher must have a kind of fire shut up in his bones and whenever injustice is around he must tell it. Somehow a preacher must be an Amos who says, 'When God speaks who can but prophesy!' And as Amos said, 'Let justice roll down like waters and righteousness like a mighty stream.' Somehow the preacher must say with Jesus, 'The spirit of the Lord is upon me, because He has anointed me!'"

It is the power of great ideas and the anointing of the Holy Spirit that have inspired people and nations to confidence and wholehearted effort during danger and hardship. Those who are possessed with great ideas and with messages from God are undaunted by hunger, pain, persecution, torture, or the threat of death. They are willing to give their lives for the cause they so ardently proclaim. They are heroes who stand as watchmen on the watchtowers of liberty, who as the Lord reminds us through the prophet Isaiah "refuse to be silent day or night."

If we love God and have a reverential fear of Him, we won't fear anything else. Just what does that reverent fear of God entail? The Lord explains it through the prophet Ezekiel:

> Son of man, give your people this message: When the watchman sees the sword coming, he sounds the alarm to warn the people. Then if those who hear the alarm refuse to take action, it is their own fault if they die. They heard the alarm but ignored it, so the responsibility is theirs. If they had listened to the warning, they could have saved their lives.
>
> But if the watchman sees the sword coming and doesn't sound the alarm to warn the people, he is responsible for their captivity. They will die in their sins, but I will hold the watchman responsible for their deaths.
>
> Now, son of man, I am making you a watchman for the people of Israel. Therefore, listen to what I say and warn them for me. If I announce that some wicked people are sure to die and you fail to tell them to change their ways, then they will die in their sins, and I will hold you responsible for their deaths. But if you warn them to repent and they don't repent, they will die in their sins, but you will have saved yourself. (Eze. 33:1-9)

If you would like to be a good speaker and deliver messages from God, regardless of your occupation or field of service - and yes, God does have thoughts on a wide range of subjects - there are certain qualifications you must meet. God anointed

Ezekiel and called him to take a message to Israel. Here is what God said to him:

> "Stand up, son of man," said the voice. "I want to speak with you." The Spirit came into me as He spoke, and He set me on my feet. I listened carefully to His words. "Son of man," he said, "I am sending you to the nation of Israel, a rebellious nation that has rebelled against me. They are a stubborn and hard hearted people. But I am sending you to say to them, 'This is what the Sovereign Lord says!' And whether they listen or refuse to listen, at least they will know they have had a prophet among them.

> "Son of man, do not fear them or their words. Don't be afraid even though their threats surround you like nettles and briers and stinging scorpions. Do not be dismayed by their dark scowls, even though they are rebels. You must give them my messages whether they listen or not ... Don't be rebellious like them.

> "Behold, I have made your face strong against their faces, and your forehead strong against their foreheads. Like adamant stone, harder than flint, I have made your forehead; do not be afraid of them, nor be dismayed at their looks." (Ezek. 2:2-8; 3:8-9)

As we read this passage from Ezekiel, we can't help but recognize this "forehead like flint" as a characteristic of the speakers we have looked at so far.

Seven

Some of the Bible's Great Messengers

The Speech Delivered in Front of the Golden Idol

King Nebuchadnezzar made a golden statue ninety feet high and nine feet wide. As the King looked out over the crowd, he was pleased that all the people in the kingdom had fallen on their faces to worship before his statue. As he glanced across the crowd, his guards pointed out three young men standing up among the bowed multitude. His happiness suddenly turned to anger. "Who do those people think they are? Guards bring them here at once!"

The three young men who had refused to bow down and worship the golden image were Hebrews who lived by the commandments of God. Their God had commanded, "You must not make an idol of any kind or an image of anything in the heavens or on the earth or in the sea. You must not bow down to them or worship them, for I, the Lord your God, am a jealous God who will not tolerate your affection for any other gods." Along with His commandment forbidding idol worship, God had given their fathers a warning and a promise, "I lay the sins of the parents upon their children; the entire family is affected—even children in the third and fourth generations of those who reject me. But I lavish unfailing love for a thousand generations on those who love me and obey my commands." What a God, what a warning, what a promise!

Yes, these young men knew God's commandments well. When they heard of the King's plans, they discussed what they were going to do, "Our God, who we worship, commanded us not to bow down before idols. He announced His commandments to our fathers from a mountain that was burning with fire, with thunder, lightning, and loud blasts from the trumpets of heaven. The whole mountain quaked at His presence. Our fathers told us that the majesty of God was so overwhelming that even Moses said he was trembling with fear. The only reason we are captives in Babylon right now is because our nation refused to obey God and got involved in idolatry. They refused to give the land a Sabbath rest, as God had instructed." They agreed among themselves, "There is no way we are going to disobey Him now."

As they stood in front of the idol, these three young men knew what they had to do. Now that they faced certain death, they had no decision to make. They had already settled the issue long before in their hearts. When the king sounded the trumpet for everyone to bow down, they stood silently and refused to bow.

Silently with their trust in God, they watched as the guards made their way toward them through the crowd that was groveling before the golden idol the King had set up. The guards promptly arrested them and brought them to the King. When King Nebuchadnezzar saw that it was Shadrach, Meshach, and Abednego, he flew into a rage. "What is the meaning of this," he demanded. "I put you in charge of the Province of Babylon. I promoted you over the other

Babylonian youth. So this is your thanks!" The young men didn't answer.

"On the other hand," the King thought to himself as he tried to regain his composure, "these are some of the best men in my kingdom. They have been better to me than all the other young men of Babylon put together. What should I do? In order to maintain control of the people, I can't allow this insubordination." Then he thought of an idea. Maybe they didn't understand that it was an order that everyone present had to bow down.

"I will give you boys one more chance," said the King. "We will strike up the band one more time. When you hear the sound of the musical instruments, bow down and worship the statue I have made. But if you refuse, you will be thrown immediately into the blazing furnace. And then what god will be able to rescue you from my power?"

Shadrach, Meshach, and Abednego replied, "King Nebuchadnezzar, we don't need to defend ourselves before you. If we are thrown into the blazing furnace, the God whom we serve is able to save us. He will rescue us from your power, Your Majesty. But even if He doesn't, we want to make it clear to you, Your Majesty, that we will never serve your gods or worship the gold statue you have set up." [62]

The King was so angry at their insubordination that his face was distorted. He ordered the oven to be heated seven times hotter and then told the soldiers to throw the three young men into the flames. The oven was so hot that the soldiers who threw the boys into the furnace dropped dead from getting too close to the fire.

Although Nebuchadnezzar knew he would be sorry in the morning, he looked at the fiery oven thinking how glad he was that these young men got what they deserved. As he gazed at the fire flaming in the oven, he suddenly jumped up in amazement and exclaimed to his advisers, "Didn't we tie up three men and throw them into the furnace? Look!" he shouted. "I see four men, unbound, walking around in the fire unharmed, and the fourth looks like a god!" The King got as close to the oven as he could and shouted for the boys to come out.

The young men came out and stood peacefully before him without even a singe on the hem of their garments. Overwhelmed with such a miracle, Nebuchadnezzar called the people from the province that were assembled before him to attention, "Praise to the God of Shadrach, Meshach, and Abednego! He sent his angel to rescue His servants who trusted in Him. They defied my command and were willing to die rather than serve or worship any god except their own God. Therefore, I make this decree: If any people, whatever their race or nation or language, speak a word against the God of Shadrach, Meshach, and Abednego, they will be torn limb from limb, and their houses will be turned into heaps of rubble. There is no other god who can rescue like this!" Then the King promoted Shadrach, Meshach, and Abednego to even higher positions in the province of Babylon. (Dan. 2)

The soldiers who threw these three young men in the flames were not able to withstand the fiery ordeal, so they met death. Yet, it was in the fire that the three young men met God face to face. They came out of the fire without even the smell of smoke. When you take a stand for Truth, no matter what the cost - whether life or death - you can rest assured that you will never be alone.

Daniel, The Confession that Spoke Volumes

Time passed and Babylon had a new King - King Darius. Daniel worked for the King and had been promoted over other Babylonians because of the excellent spirit that was in him. Daniel had a zeal for God just like the three young Jewish men that Nebuchadnezzar had thrown in the fire. And why shouldn't he? After all, Daniel had been their mentor and teacher.

The other men who worked under the King were so jealous that they laid a plot to try to destroy Daniel. They got Darius to sign a law that people should worship and pray to no one but the King. When Daniel knew that King Darius had signed the document, Daniel entered his house and prayed by his open window so everyone in Babylon could see him. Three times a day Daniel prayed and gave thanks to God as he had done previously. Daniel was a man called to deliver the message that no god was to be worshiped except the Holy One of Israel. Like his three friends, he refused to let that message go, even in the face of death. Because Daniel honored God above all else, he did not fear the King's edict.

When news reached King Darius that Daniel was praying to his God, Darius was grieved. The men who were jealous of Daniel insisted that the King was bound by law to throw Daniel into the den of lions for his disobedience. So the King was forced to do what he didn't want to do, and had Daniel thrown to the lions. Daniel had given such a powerful testimony to King Darius over the years that as Daniel was being taken away to the lions' den, the King called out after him, "Daniel, the God whom you serve continually will deliver you from the mouth of the lions." What a testimony Daniel had given to a heathen king!

"A stone was brought and placed over the mouth of the den. The King sealed the stone with his own royal seal and the seals of his nobles, so that no one could rescue Daniel. Then the King returned to his palace and spent the night fasting. He refused his usual entertainment and couldn't sleep at all that night" because he was so worried about Daniel. Early in the morning, the King ran to the lions' den to see if Daniel's God had rescued him.   "Daniel, servant of the living God," King Darius called out, "has your God, whom you serve continually, been able to deliver you from the lions?"

Daniel answered, "Long live the King! My God sent his angel to shut the lions' mouths so that they would not hurt me, for I have been found innocent in His sight. And I have not wronged you, Your Majesty."

The King was overjoyed and ordered that Daniel be lifted from the den. When King Darius saw that Daniel was alive and

Daniel's Answer to the King by Briton Rivière

there was not a scratch on him because he trusted in God, he made the following decree: "From this day on, everyone in my kingdom must fear the God of Daniel, because there was no other God like Him, He is the Living God whose kingdom is forever!"   Then he ordered the men who had plotted against Daniel and maliciously accused him to be thrown into the lion's den along with their wives and children. The lions tore them to bits before they could hit the floor. Daniel's bold stand for Truth, regardless of the personal cost, won a heathen king to the Lord, and brought a nation face to face with the Living God. Daniel's testimony changed things. (Dan. 6)

The Apostles, the Christian martyrs, the great revivalists, and Christian statesmen throughout history have had this same tenacity in their confrontation with evil. Through their great confessions and bold proclamation of the Truth, they have changed the destinies of individuals and entire nations.

The Sermon from the Church's First Martyr

Stephen, a deacon in the early church, was full of the Holy Spirit and power. One day some Jews from the synagogue tried to debate with Stephen, but "none of them could stand against the wisdom and the Spirit with which Stephen spoke." The men were so jealous of Stephen that they made up lies saying that Stephen was blaspheming. The religious leaders arrested Stephen and brought him before the council. "At this point," the Scriptures tell us, "everyone in the high council stared at Stephen, because his face became as bright as an angel's." The Jewish leaders asked Stephen to give an account of what he had been teaching. Stephen started with God's call on Abraham and went through the Hebrew Scriptures speaking of Jacob, Joseph, Moses, Joshua, David, and Solomon. Then he said this:

"You stubborn people! You are heathen at heart and deaf to the truth. Must you forever resist the Holy Spirit? That's what your ancestors did, and so do you! Name one prophet your ancestors didn't persecute! They even killed the ones who predicted the coming of the Righteous One, the Messiah whom you betrayed and murdered. You deliberately disobeyed God's law, even though you received it from the hands of angels." The Jews began to shake their fists at him in rage. Full of the Holy Spirit, Stephen cried out, "Behold, I see heaven opened and the Son of Man standing at the right hand of God!" (Acts 7)

Martyrdom of St Stephen *as Saul (Paul) Looks On-* *Rembrandt*

What boldness! The stones started flying, but Stephen's face was set like flint as he stood firmly in the blaze of Truth. Although Stephen met physical death for his bold preaching, Jesus stood up from His throne to welcome him into the realms of glory.

Everyone Called to Preach the Gospel

When Jesus rose from the dead, He gathered His disciples and said to them, "Go into all the world and make disciples of all nations, teaching them to obey everything that I have taught you." And then He told them, "Go to Jerusalem and wait for the promise of the Father. You will receive power when the Holy Spirit comes upon you, and you will be my witnesses." And, oh yes, He left them another promise. He told them they would never be alone - "I will be with you always," Jesus promised, "even until the end of the world." What a God! What a promise!

Jesus gave this Great Commission, not only to those who walked and talked with Him on earth, but to all who would be His followers throughout all the ages, for all time to come. This commission and these promises from Jesus our Savior, call me to throw out my self-centered thoughts and my narrow self-conscious mindset, and to fix my whole attention, not on myself, but on Christ and His power and Presence within me. His commission and His promises call me to be determined to fill my mind with the highest thoughts that I can think and to cast out every negative, fearful, and doubtful thought that exalts itself above the knowledge of God and His Word. I must learn to think God's thoughts after Him - until my mind and soul catch fire.

Rising to the Challenge

In the earliest biblical accounts, we find God always calling and challenging people to do His will. When Moses encountered the Great I Am in the burning bush, God challenged him to stretch his mind and grasp one of the greatest ideas ever presented to man. After Moses had taken off his shoes because of the Holy Presence in the bush that had sanctified the ground, God said, "I have seen the affliction of

My people who are in Egypt, and I have surely given heed to their cry because of their taskmasters, for I am aware of their sufferings .... Therefore, come now, and I will send you to Pharaoh, so that you may bring My people, the sons of Israel, out of Egypt."

But Moses said, "Who am I, that I should go to Pharaoh, and that I should bring the sons of Israel out of Egypt?"

God answered, "Certainly I will be with you." Yet, in spite of the stunning vision and the majesty of God's Holy Presence, Moses was still focused on himself. He could not grasp the magnitude of what God had just promised.

The God of heaven and earth had promised to go with him, yet, Moses was still not on focusing on who God was, but on his own personal inadequacy. Moses had that sick, weak in the knees feeling. As Moses lay prostrate before the burning bush, he probably struggled with the thoughts that flooded his mind - "When I fled from Egypt, Pharaoh was searching everywhere for me so he could execute me for murder. Surely someone there will recognize me. How can I go back now as a wanted man to deliver a multitude. Besides, even though I was trained in all the warfare of Egypt, and I once knew how to marshal forces, I have no army to command. Anyway, I have forgotten everything I learned over the forty years I have been a shepherd in the wilderness."

Moses lifted his head slightly and pleaded with the Lord, "O Lord, I'm not very good with words. I never have been, and I'm not now, even though You have spoken to me. I get tongue-tied, and my words get tangled."

Then the Lord asked Moses, "Who makes a person's mouth? Who decides whether people speak or do not speak, hear or do not hear, see or do not see? Is it not I, the Lord? Now go! I will be with you as you speak, and I will instruct you in what to say."

Moses couldn't shake his fear. "Please, Lord," he pleaded, "send the message by somebody else."

Then the anger of the Lord burned against Moses, and He said, "Is there not your brother Aaron the Levite? I know that he speaks fluently ... speak to him and put the words in his mouth, and I will be with your mouth and his mouth, and I will teach you what you are to do." (Ex. 3:7, 10, 11-15)

In the beginning of God's call upon his life, Moses was not able to fathom this great idea of delivering millions of enslaved people from the hand of Pharaoh with simple words and supernatural signs. God was not happy with Moses' unbelief, but was kind enough to provide a helper for Moses to stand with him.

As their talks with Pharaoh continued, and God faithfully brought the plagues upon Egypt which He had promised, Moses cast aside his fearful, self-centered thoughts. From spending so much time communing with God, Moses became so on fire with God's message that he no longer waited for Aaron to speak for him; he was free from fear, he spoke to Pharaoh directly without fear or intimidation.

Jeremiah - Called to Speak for God

When God called Jeremiah to be a prophet to the nations, he, too, at first was overcome with self-centered thoughts. Jeremiah said, "O Sovereign Lord, I can't speak for you! I'm too young!"

The Lord replied, "Don't say, 'I'm too young,' for you must go wherever I send you and say whatever I tell you. And don't be afraid of the people, for I will be with you and will protect you. I, the Lord, have spoken! ... Get up and prepare for action. Go out and tell them everything I tell you to say. Do not be afraid of them, or I will make you look foolish in front of them." (Jer. 1: 6-8, 17)

Jeremiah, perhaps having learned from Moses' initial failure to trust in God's call, decided to believe God. He was set free from fear and his self-centered thoughts and went in faith to speak to the people all that God told him. However, Jeremiah's message was so unpopular that later he reflected, "The word of the Lord has resulted in reproach and derision all day long. But if I say, 'I will not remember Him or speak any more in His name, then in my heart it becomes like a burning fire shut up in my bones; and I am weary of holding it in, and I cannot endure it ... the Lord is with me like a dread

The Prophet Jeremiah
From the *Sistine Chapel* *by Michelangelo*

champion." (Jer. 20:8c-9, 11) Jeremiah had become so aflame with God's message that he could not be silent; even when he tried to hold it in, he could not be quiet, even when it meant that he would be mocked and ridiculed because of what he said. He was a man so possessed by his calling and the message he had heard from God that he was able to move out of his self-centered thoughts and fix his attention upon the highest thoughts a man can think - the Word of God. Jesus said it this way, "Therefore do not fear them. For there is nothing covered that will not be revealed, and hidden that will not be known. Whatever I tell you in the dark, speak in the light; and what you hear in the ear, preach on the housetops. And do not fear those who kill the body but cannot kill the soul. But rather fear Him who is able to destroy both soul and body in hell." (Matt. 10:26-18)

The Prophets' Secret

In the year that King Uzziah died, Isaiah saw the Lord in His glory. Isaiah records that he saw the Lord high and lifted up, and the train of His robe filled the temple. Angels were flying around his head crying, "Holy, holy, holy, the whole earth is filled with His glory!" The whole temple filled with smoke from His glory, and then Isaiah said, "It's all over! I am doomed, for I am a sinful man. I have filthy lips, and I live among a people with filthy lips. Yet, I have seen the King, the Lord of Heaven's Armies." An angel touched his lips with a burning coal from off the altar and purified his lips. Then Isaiah heard the Lord say, "Whom shall I send? Who will go for me?" Isaiah answered, "Here am I, Lord, send me." (Isa. 6)

The book of Isaiah reveals the secret of effective service: "The Lord God has given me the tongue of disciples, that I may know how to sustain the weary one with a word. He awakens me morning by morning, He awakens my ear to listen as a disciple. The Lord God has opened my ear; and I was not disobedient, nor did I turn back."(Is. 50:4, 5)

Ability to speak comes from the practice of listening intently to the voice of the Lord and obediently telling the words that God gives you to say and doing what God tells you to do. Jeremiah shares the same secret:

> Then the Lord said, "Who has stood in the council of the Lord that he should see and hear His word? Who has given heed to His word and listened? ... I did not send these prophets, but they ran. I did not speak to them, but they prophesied. But, if they had stood in My counsel, then they would have announced My words to My people, and would have turned them back from their evil way and from the evil of their deeds .... Is not My word like fire?" declares the Lord, "and like a hammer which shatters a rock?" (Jer. 23:18, 21, 29)

From these passages, we can clearly see that the power to move the hearts of men lies in seeking God, standing in His counsel, and proclaiming His words to the world. As I spend time in His Presence and listen to His voice, my heart will burn with His word, and my thoughts will burst into flame with God's ideas.

In 1817, John A. Broadus pointed out the underlying theme of good speeches in his classic book *The Preparation and Delivery of Sermons*: "True Christian preaching is not a message about God, it is a message from God!"

David once made this bold speech to a Philistine giant: "You come to me with sword, spear, and javelin, but I come to you in the name of the LORD of Heaven's Armies - the God of the armies of Israel, whom you have defied!" Later, as a psalmist, David made this observation: "My heart was hot within me; while I was musing the fire burned; then I spoke with my tongue." (Samuel 17:45; Ps.39:3)

It was while musing that the fire began to burn within David's soul and caused him to speak boldly and get supernatural results.

To *muse*, according to *Webster's 1828 Dictionary*, means "to ponder; to think closely, to study in silence, to be so occupied in study or contemplation as not to observe passing scenes or things present."

As I take time to wait in the presence of God and study God's Word, my mind will be lifted up to think God's thoughts. As I muse upon these thoughts, rolling them over and over in my mind, thinking and pondering on the things that God is putting in my heart, my soul will catch fire and with messages from God.

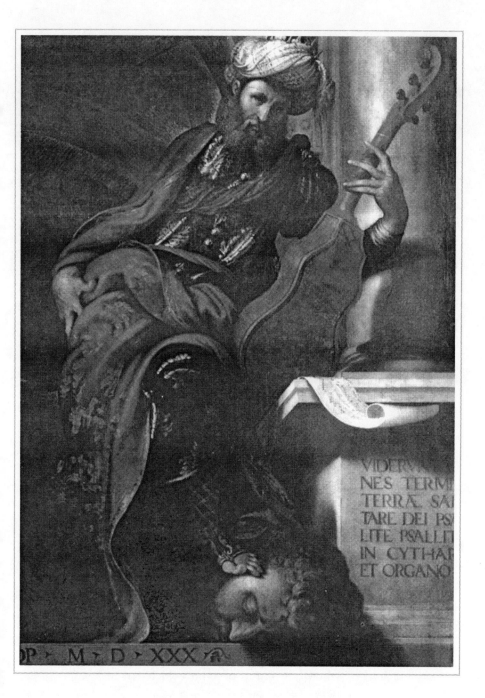

The Prophet David *by Camillo Boccaccio*

Eight

How to Master Your Thoughts

There is one thing that you may have recognized about all the speakers we have considered. Each one of them spent lots of time in reading and study. Charles Spurgeon was one of the last great Puritan preachers in Britain in the 19th-century. It is estimated that during his lifetime he spoke in person to over ten million people. This was of course was long before television. Often his sermons were transcribed as he spoke and were translated into many different languages.

Charles Haddon Spurgeon - 1834-1892

Spurgeon was a prolific author, and his skills in oratory often held his audience spellbound. Spurgeon makes this note:

> In 1857, a day or two before preaching at the Crystal Palace, I went to decide where the platform should be fixed; and, in order to test the acoustic properties of the building, cried in a loud voice, "Behold the Lamb of God, which taketh away the sin of the world." In one of the galleries, a workman,

who knew nothing of what was being done, heard the words, and they came like a message from heaven to his soul. He was smitten with conviction on account of sin, put down his tools, went home, and there, after a season of spiritual struggling, found peace and life by beholding the Lamb of God. Years after, he told this story to one who visited him on his death-bed.[63]

Spurgeon gave the following advice to all those who came to him and wanted to know the art of being a great

Charles Spurgeon Preaching at Surrey Gardens Music Hall
Kennington, England

communicator:

Extemporary speech without study is a cloud without rain. Out of nothing comes nothing. If we can study and do not, we have no right to call in a Divine agent to make up the deficits of our idleness or eccentricity.

The God of Providence has promised to feed His people with temporal food; but if we came together to a banquet, and no one had prepared a single dish, because all had faith in the Lord that food would be given in the same hour, the festival would not be eminently satisfactory but folly would be rebuked by hunger ...

All sermons ought to be well considered and prepared by the preachers; and as much as possible, every minister should, with much prayer for heavenly guidance, enter fully into his subject, exert all his mental faculties in original thinking, and gather together all the information within his reach.

His sermon should be his mental life-blood, the out-flow of his intellectual and spiritual vigor ... his words should be diamonds well cut and well set - precious, intrinsically, and bearing the marks of labor. God forbid that we should offer to the Lord that which costs us nothing. [64]

Spurgeon, "Heaven and Hell": https://goo.gl/zZ63be

Spurgeon: "Fellowship with Christ":
https://goo.gl/3Dbyyj

Louis M. Bautain's classic work of the nineteenth-century, *The Art of Extempore Speaking*, has been said to have no counterpart or rival in the English language. Bautain recognizes two types of speaking - prepared speaking and being compelled to speak by overwhelming passion. First, there is prepared extempore speaking - a speech to be delivered in public before a specific audience on a certain day about a given subject. In preparation for this type of speech, Bautain gives this advice:

You will never be capable of speaking properly in public unless you acquire such mastery of your own thought as to be able to decompose it into its parts, to analyze it into its elements and then recompose, re-gather and concentrate it again ... the pen is the scalpel which dissects the thoughts and never, except when you write down what you behold internally, can you succeed in clearly discerning all that is contained in a conception, or in obtaining its well-marked scope. You then will be able to understand yourself, and make others understand you.[65]

Let's review Bautain's advice from the paragraph above:

1. Use your pen to analyze your thoughts.

2. Dissect your thoughts. Break your thoughts down into parts.

3. Write down what you behold internally.

4. Discern all that is contained in your idea - (there is a lot you will not discern about your subject, until you take time to write down all the aspects as they present themselves to you.)

5. Recompose the parts back into a whole.

The second type of speaking is the exceptional case when a person is so excited by passion that speech "bursts forth like a burning volcano scattering fire and lava or like a sudden storm evoking lighting, thunder, and rain." Bautain writes, "No advice can be given in such a situation for nature alone furnishes the means ... there lies the source of all poetry, of all eloquence, of all artists' power. Improvisation such as this recognizes no rules, and rejects teaching. The coarsest, the most ignorant man may thus occasionally be eloquent, if he feel vividly and express himself energetically, in words and gesture."[66]

Examples of this type of speaking can be seen in Peter's speech on the day of Pentecost, Stephen before the religious leaders, Patrick Henry in his *Call to Arms*, Daniel Webster when he expounded the greatness of the U.S. Constitution before his classmates, Martin Luther when he spoke before the Diet at Worms, Martin Luther King when he gave his *I have a Dream Speech*, Shadrach, Mesheck and Abednego who were called before King Nebuchadnezzar when they refused to bow down to his golden idol, and David when he challenged Goliath. Included in the second group of speakers are also those who are often called on to make a speech at a moment's notice such as a preacher, a professor, or a senator. These usually speak out of their fulness, and having meditated at length upon their subject, they are able to bring their ideas out and develop them before their audience. Bautain refers to this as a kind of "child bearing" in public.

Regardless of which type of speaking you are more suited for, your speech should never be something you have simply memorized and are just quoting. When you have mastered your thoughts in private and then have the opportunity to speak in public, you will always be ready to give a talk on the subject. The fire you carry in your heart will burst forth. Your speech will be fresh and warm and will be communicated with fervor to your audience.

But, if you do not keep the inner fire burning, you will not be able to speak from the heart, and you will come across like an extinct volcano whose celestial fire has gone out. "If the ax is dull, you must exert more strength," the ancient Hebrew King reminds us. However, an ax of the intellect sharpened and polished through meditation, prayer and study, has the power to give success. (Proverbs 10:10)

The Art of Extempore Speaking by Bautain, 1921 edition, can be read online - Highly Recommended: https://goo.gl/ZmFiZ7

The Apostle Paul Reveals His Secret

"There is a spirit of intelligence within man," says Job, "but the inspiration of the Almighty gives the understanding." (Job 32:8)

Paul knew this all too well. While he was persecuting the early church and presiding over their arrest and execution as heretics, he was blinded by the Light from heaven. He would later tell the church, "the natural mind cannot understand spiritual things - they are *spiritually discerned.*" Then in these unforgettable words, Paul explains how the Holy Spirit teaches:

"These things we also speak, not in words which man's wisdom teaches but which the Holy Spirit teaches, comparing spiritual things with spiritual." He encouraged the church to always be sure to ask God for revelation from the Holy Spirit. Paul would have us understand that it is not by thinking harder and longer that we come to understand spiritual things - spiritual things must be revealed to us by God's Holy Spirit as we study spiritual words and compare them with each other and ask God for revelation and understanding.

Conversion of Saul by Gustave Dore

Eye has not seen, nor ear heard, nor have entered into the heart of man. The things which God has prepared for those who love Him. But God has revealed them to us through His Spirit. For the Spirit searches all things, yes, the deep things of God. For what man knows the things of a man except the spirit of the man which is in him? Even so, no one knows the things of God except the Spirit of God. Now we have received, not the spirit of the world, but the Spirit who is from God, that we might know the things that have been freely given to us by God. (2 Cor. 2:9-12)

The Prayer that Can Change Everything

Nothing is more effective than to pray the Bible's own prayers that have been inspired by the Holy Spirit. One of the best prayers to pray for the Holy Spirit's revelation is Paul's great prayer for the church in Ephesians. Here it is:

I do not cease to make mention of you in my prayers, that the God of our Lord Jesus Christ, the Father of glory, may give to you the spirit of wisdom and revelation in the knowledge of Him, the eyes of your understanding being enlightened; that you may know what is the hope of His calling, what are the riches of the glory of His inheritance in the saints, and what is the exceeding greatness of His power toward us who believe, according to the working of His mighty power which He worked in Christ when He raised Him from the dead and seated at His right hand in the heavenly places. (Ephes. 1:16-20)

One of the great teachers of faith of the twentieth century, Kenneth Hagin, tells of the success he had from praying the great prayers of the Bible. In a small church where he was the pastor, he decided that every time he passed by the front of the sanctuary, he would kneel at the altar and pray

Paul's prayer for revelation from Ephesians. He did this everyday for a few minutes, six times a day. He relates that by the end of the first two weeks, he had so much revelation from God he could hardly get it all down.

After he had done this faithfully for two years, something happened he had never thought possible. The Lord began to appear to him and personally gave him all the revelation on faith which he preached that has blessed the body of Christ throughout the world. His message has lifted believers up to new heights of spirituality, blessing, and anointing to do exploits for the kingdom of God. This does not necessarily mean that if you do the same thing as he did faithfully for two years that you will see the Lord with your natural eyes, although you may. The main point of the story is that you can be sure you will receive revelation from God - you will feast on "hidden manna." There is nothing more delightful than this.

But if you do not ask, most likely you won't receive much. James, Jesus' very own flesh and blood brother, reminds us, "You have not because you ask not." (4:2) There are immeasurable blessings and insights that Christians forfeit because they do not ask for God's blessings in prayer. Jesus told His disciples, "Ask and you shall receive, seek and you shall find, knock and the door shall be opened ... Up until now you have asked for nothing in My name. Ask so that you may receive so your joy may be full." (Luke 11:9, John 16:24) From my own testimony, I can say that I have proved Paul's prayer for revelation from God to be true.

If you will faithfully and consistently pray this prayer, a whole new understanding of the scriptures and spiritual things will be open to you. This insight and understanding is not limited to biblical revelation. God will give you revelation and insight on any subject or about any field of endeavor in which you are seeking for help. This is the source of the "Aha!"

moment. Once you were blind but now you see. Once you did not understand something - now a light goes on and you fully understand it. This was accomplished not because you finally thought so hard you figured it out, but because you received insight and enlightenment from God.

The Importance of Study and Meditation

Many Christians fail to spend time in prayer and study because of a misinterpretation of Scripture. Jesus told His disciples, "They will lay their hands on you and will persecute you, delivering you to the synagogues and prison, bringing you before kings and governors for My name's sake. It will lead to an opportunity for your testimony. So make up your minds not to prepare beforehand to defend yourselves; for I will give you words and wisdom which none of your opponents will be able to resist or refute." (Luke 21:12-15)

It is important to notice that in this passage that Jesus is not telling His disciples to avoid prayer or study before they speak publicly. He is referring to a time of persecution in which they may be called up before authorities to defend themselves. He is telling His disciples not to worry about what they should say in their own personal defense, or their defense of the Gospel. He will give them the words to speak at the moment they need to be spoken.

We see this spiritual promise working when John Huss, Martin Luther, and Stephen were brought before the religious leaders to give an account of their teaching. They spoke extemporaneously without notes. But be assured, they had spent untold hours in personal devotions - in worship, prayer, study, and meditation on God's Word. They had heard messages from God and were busy telling those messages to other people. This is what got them into trouble and aroused the anger of the religious councils. The ancient Hebrew King offers this advise:

> Make your ear attentive to wisdom, incline your heart to understanding, if you seek her as silver, and search for her as for hidden treasures; then you will discern the fear of the Lord and discover the knowledge of God. For the Lord gives wisdom; from His mouth come knowledge and understanding ... for wisdom will enter your heart and knowledge will be pleasant to your soul; discretion will guard you, understanding will watch over you. (Prov. 2: 1-6, 10-11)

So, never forget that in order to overflow, to speak extemporaneously, your heart must be full. Jesus reminds us that it is "out of the abundance of the heart the mouth will speak." (Luke 6:45) Get in the habit of feeding your mind with food for thought. Store your mind with rich thoughts. These thoughts can be found in the Bible, in Christian writings, in true accounts of history, in scientific studies, in great literature, in inspired poetry. And yes, don't forget to read or listen to the speeches of great orators. Study the speeches of great statesmen and great Christian leaders - America's Founding Fathers, Patrick Henry, George Washington, John Adams, Daniel Webster, Charles Spurgeon, Abraham Lincoln, John Wesley, Charles Finney, Catherine Booth, Elizabeth Caddy Stanton, Margaret Thatcher, Dr. Martin Luther King, Ronald Reagan.

A collection of speeches worth studying can be found at these websites:

American Rhetoric: http://www.americanrhetoric.com/

35 of the Greatest Speeches in History: https://goo.gl/6JSqtw

Top 100 Free Motivational Speeches from **Learnoutloud:** https://goo.gl/Kex3Mu

Collection of Speeches by Dr. Martin Luther King from Learnoutloud: https://goo.gl/kKhVx5

Collection of Historic Christian Sermons: https://goo.gl/VkNuiy

Importance of Content

If you are called on to make a speech, don't waste time all week and then cast yourself upon the Lord for His aid. This is presumption. We cannot expect the Lord to cover up for our self-indulgence and slothfulness. Nor should we impose ourselves on people who have taken their time to listen by offering them a "grain of wheat for a gallon of water." Good delivery may make your speech lively, but without content it will not be deep. It will be like clouds without water, and never be able to bring up fruit or flower. You may enjoy hearing yourself talk, but no one really profits from it.

Scripture reminds us, "In the multitude of words there is great transgression. The words of the wise are like goads, and the words of scholars are like well-driven nails, given by one Shepherd." (Eccl. 12: 11) One of the greatest exercises to become astute at this is to have to speak on the mission field to people of a different language.

If you have an hour to speak and the translation takes half of the hour, it is amazing how many unnecessary words you can eliminate from your message so that only the important things are said. You may not have the opportunity to speak to a foreign audience, but you can imagine that you do. Go back over your talk and take out the unnecessary words, which often may tire your hearers. They do not necessarily need three or four stories to drive home one point. More often than not, "A word to the wise is sufficient."

A.W. Tozer, known by many as a twentieth-century prophet, had this to say about the importance of content:

I take my help where I can find it and always graze where the pastures are greenest. Only one stipulation do I make: my teacher must know God, otherwise than by hearsay, and Christ must be all and all to him. If a man has only correct doctrine to offer me, I am sure to slip out at the first intermission to seek the company of someone who has seen for himself how lovely is the Rose of Sharon and the Lily of the Valley. Such a man can help me and no one else. [67]

It is one thing to have heard a flute sweetly played and tell people what you have heard by first hand experience. It is another thing to tell something second hand and repeat someone else's account of how the flute sounded or of what you have read in a Bible concordance. Are you a parrot in your speaking? Do you repeat and parrot a message God gave to someone else or is that message alive and real to you?

Bautain writes about what it is like to speak from truth that has been made real to us:

> When we perceive a truth, the mind rejoices and feeds upon it....the mind partakes of its expansive force, and experiences a desire of announcing to others what it knows, and of making them see what it sees. It is its happiness to become a torch of this light and to help in diffusing it. It sometimes glories in the joy it feels. [68]

If your words come from Divine inspiration, they will pierce hearts and do what God has sent them to do. That is His promise from His Word. However, never think that because you are a good speaker that this alone gives your words power.

When Abraham Lincoln spoke at Gettysburg to commemorate the battle of the Civil War and the men who fought and died there, he was not the featured speaker of the day. That honor went to Edward Everett, a very famous orator

Lincoln at Gettysburg by Fletcher Cransom

and statesman. At this time in our nation's history, listening to oratory was a national past time. If the oration wasn't at least two hours long, people felt the orator wasn't worth much. People of that era loved speeches. (And to tell you the truth, I think people still love speeches today - the problem is that speakers with content and meaning that are worth listening to are sometimes hard to come by.)

The celebration commemorating Gettysburg was replete with speeches. On the night before the ceremony, the streets were filled with musical bands and cheering people calling for impromptu speeches from the dignitaries that were in town for the ceremonies. The next day at the battlefield Edward Everett delivered his oration to an adoring crowd, holding the audience spellbound for two hours. Then it was President Lincoln's turn. His speech came to be known as *The Gettysburg Address*. Here it is in its entirety:

Fourscore and seven years ago our fathers brought forth on this continent a new nation, conceived in liberty and dedicated to the proposition that all men are created equal. Now we are engaged in a great civil war, testing whether that nation or any nation so conceived and so dedicated can long endure.

We are met on a great battlefield of that war. We have come to dedicate a portion of that field as a final resting place for those who gave their lives that that nation might live. It is altogether fitting and proper that we should do this.

But in a larger sense, we cannot dedicate, we cannot consecrate, we cannot hallow this ground. The brave men, living and dead who struggled here, have consecrated it far above our poor power to add or detract. The world will little note nor long remember what we say here, but it can never forget what they did here.

It is for us the living rather to be dedicated here to the unfinished work which they who fought here have thus far so nobly advanced. It is rather for us to be here dedicated to the great task remaining before us - that from these honored dead we take increased devotion to that cause for which they gave the last full measure of devotion - that we here highly resolve that these dead shall not have died in vain, that this nation, under God, shall have a new birth of freedom, and that government of the people, by the people, for the people shall not perish from the earth.

The speech lasted about two minutes. No one remembers what the great orator Edward Everett said that day - in fact very few people even know his name - but the words of Abraham Lincoln have gone down in history. E.W. Andrews, the aide of a Union general, sat near the speakers' platform. Commenting on Lincoln's speech, Andrews said, "The great assembly listened almost awestruck as if to a voice from the divine oracle."

Everett wrote Lincoln a brief note the next day requesting a copy of the speech and covering it with praise: "Permit me also to express my great admiration of the thoughts expressed by you, with such eloquent simplicity and appropriateness, at the consecration of the cemetery. I should be glad, if I could flatter myself that I came as near to the central idea of the occasion, in two hours, as you did in two minutes."[69]

Lincoln's Advice

Despite popular stories, historians agree that Lincoln did not whip up his "remarks" on the back of an envelope en-route from Washington. His effort was the product of a lifetime from a man known for study and deep reflection. He wrote at least half or more of his address on White House stationery before his trip, and apparently applied finishing touches in his room at the Wills House the night before the ceremonies. Lincoln went to great lengths to get to Gettysburg, even though sickness threatened to keep him from coming. He had already lost two children to disease, and he knew sickness wasn't something you played with.

But Lincoln was determined to get to Gettysburg. He felt he must say a few remarks to cement the nation's commitment to the war efforts and the cause of the Union. The speech was so well-loved that Lincoln was asked to reproduce handwritten copies to use to sell to help support widows of the fallen soldiers. Lincoln had to get the newspaper for a copy of the speech to see exactly what he had said because he had ad-libbed some of the comments and had not written them in his original version.

The work behind Lincoln's oratorical skill can best be summed up by the following story. Once Abraham Lincoln was asked to speak for the Daughters of the American Revolution. Lincoln accepted. "When can you come?" the President of the DAR asked. "How long would you like me to speak? Lincoln replied. "What difference does it make?" she questioned. "Well," Lincoln continued, "if you want me to speak for two hours, I will be right over. But if you want me to speak for ten minutes, you need to give me at least two weeks."

Sometimes lengthy speeches are just excuses for a lack of preparation. If you have two hours to deliver your speech, hopefully you'll get around to your point, but you might wear out your audience in the process. More often than not, less is more. Cut out all the unnecessary asides, which unfortunately are often just rabbit trails a speaker takes either because he is unprepared or enjoys hearing himself talk.

If you keep your cup "full" and running over, in an emergency or on the spur of the moment when you are called upon to speak without prior knowledge or are deeply impressed that something must be said, you may with fullest confidence cast yourself upon the Lord and depend upon the Spirit of God to give you the words to say. If you have been diligent in study and have spent time listening to God speak to you, your heart should overflow with God's theme regardless of the subject matter, issue, problem, or the cause you are addressing.

Hear Lincoln's Gettysburg Address read by Jeff Daniels:
https://goo.gl/Q9Cvv3

Gettysburg Address read by Johnny Cash:
https://goo.gl/MZMGGL

Listen to the History of the Gettysburg Address from Library of Congress: http://goo.gl/BA1kN

Supernatural Aid

Spurgeon explains his experience with being a recipient of God's supernatural aid and power:

> The Divine Mind beyond a doubt comes into contact with the human intellect, lifts it out of its weakness and distraction, makes it soaring and strong and enables it both to understand and to express Divine Truth in a manner far beyond its unaided powers. Such interpositions are not meant to supersede our efforts or slacken our diligence, but are the Lord's assistance .... In every situation, we should cultivate a childlike reliance upon the Holy Ghost."[70]

The Apostle Paul explained it this way:

> And my language and my message were not set forth in persuasive enticing and plausible words of wisdom, but they were in demonstration of the Spirit and power, a proof by the Spirit and power of God operating in me and stirring in the minds of my hearers the most holy emotions and thus persuading them, so that your faith might not rest in the wisdom of men (human philosophy), but in the power of God. (2 Cor. 2:4-5 Amp)

Seventeenth century Bible commentator Matthew Henry writes about Paul's dedication to the content of his message and its Source:

> Paul did not try to appear a fine orator or a deep philosopher; nor did he insinuate himself into their minds by a flourish of words or a pompous show of deep reason and extraordinary science and skill. He did not set himself to captivate the ear by fine turns and eloquent expressions, nor to please and entertain the fancy with lofty flights of sublime notions.

Neither his speech, nor the wisdom he taught, savored of human skill: he learnt both in another school. Divine wisdom needed not to be set off with such human ornaments. He came among them declaring the testimony of God. He published a Divine revelation, and gave in sufficient vouchers for the Authority of it, both by its consonancy to ancient predictions and by present miraculous operations; and there he left the matter. Ornaments of speech and philosophical skill and argument could add no weight to what came recommended by such Authority. [71]

Nine

Some Basic Principles

We have discovered that we need to study, meditate, and analyze our thoughts. We have learned the necessity of praying for revelation from the Holy Spirit to help us expand our minds to understand great ideas and cause our hearts to be on fire with God's message. We have learned the necessity of asking God to anoint us with Power from on High. Now we will look at some practical methods of preparation and delivery. Richard C. Borden in *Public Speaking as Listeners Like It,* another classic text, offers these practical suggestions:[72]

1. Clearness in speaking is fundamental. The speaker should be content not when his meaning may be understood, but when his meaning *cannot be misunderstood*. Therefore, every speech you make must have a purpose and a form. Listeners like speeches with backbone. They dislike a "jellyfish" speech which is flabby, shapeless, begins nowhere, rambles on in all directions and ends up in the air.

2. Start your speech with a fire! Your speech is not well organized unless you are able to kindle a quick flame of spontaneous interest in the first sentence. You must introduce your subject in such a manner as to arrest the attention of your audience.

3. You must build a bridge. Don't forget that your listeners live on an island of their own interests. You must convince your listeners that your subject matters to them and is in their interest.

4. Illustrate your speech with enough concrete cases to carry conviction. Then, get down to actual cases - give them some "for instances." Listeners like to hear instances which involve famous people and history. They like examples in story form. Present them as "organized platoons in marching order." As Spurgeon says, "Never let your thoughts rush as a mob, but make them march as a troop of soldiery. Order, which is heaven's first law, must not be neglected by heaven's ambassadors."[73]

5. Do not forget to ask your audience for some specific action. In the conclusion of your speech, ask for some action or response which is in their power to give. What do you want them to do about all that you have said? Join? Contribute? Vote? Write? Boycott? Buy? Repent? Pray? Study? Work? When you feel tempted to end your speech without a request for action, remember the Chinese proverb of the Middle Ages: "To talk much and arrive nowhere is the same as climbing a tree to catch fish."

6. Look at your listeners with friendly focused eyes. If you really want to connect with your audience, you must look at your listeners as individual people, not over their heads or as one composite blur. Approach your speaking as you would a conversation. Speak to a group as you would to an individual friend in a conversation. You may have to speak louder and more intensely and vigorously, but conversation makes a good model.

A Desire to Communicate

In *Thinking and Speaking*, Walter and Scott emphasize:

Dwell as intently as possible on the meaning of what you are saying. To gain the natural responses of conversation in your speech, the practical rule is to pay no studied attention to your own voice or its inflections. Totally withdraw your thoughts from thinking about how you sound. This speech is not about you, it is about the message you are trying to communicate. Instead, trust that just as in personal conversation, you will naturally and spontaneously emphasize the proper words and phrases. If you focus on the meaning of what you are saying, not on how your words sound, your tone will flow just like it does in normal everyday conversation. What is most important is your full concentration on the content of your words as you speak them. [74]

Nothing substitutes for a deep desire to communicate your message with your audience. If you do not have a full understanding of what you are talking about, your speech will be lifeless, dull, and lacking in power. The truth is that it is only as you grasp the deep significance of your ideas that your desire to speak publicly and their consequences for good if acted upon that your ability to convince your audience will increase.

This was the motivation behind Martin Luther's determination to go and present his views before the Diet of Worms, even "if there be as many devils as there are tiles on the roof tops." We see it in Patrick Henry's oration, acclaimed to be the world's most famous cry for freedom, "Is life so dear, or peace so sweet as to be purchased at the price of chains and slavery? Forbid it, Almighty God! I know not what course others may take, but as for me, give me liberty, or give me death!" We see it in Daniel Webster's determination to defend the Constitution against unfair criticism and to help people understand it. He knew its worth and understood the consequences of losing freedom and liberty for our nation and the human race. He understood the suffering that people would have to endure if the Constitution was rejected and the Union fell apart.

We see this deep desire to communicate in Abraham Lincoln's push to get to Gettysburg to speak to the people, regardless of his illness, and in William Pitt's effort to get up off his sick bed to address the British Parliament on behalf of liberty. We see it when Elizabeth Cady Stanton spoke this on behalf of women's rights:

> We do not expect our path will be strewn with the flowers of popular applause, but over the thorns of bigotry and prejudice will be our way, and on our banner will beat the dark storm clouds of opposition from those who have entrenched themselves behind the stormy bulwarks of custom and authority... Undauntedly we will unfurl it to the gale, for we know that the storm cannot rend from it a shred, that the electric flash will but more clearly show to us the glorious words inscribed upon it, "Equality of Rights."

We see it when Martin Luther King threw caution to the wind and launched out into his "I have a dream," and made journalists take note that Something greater than Dr. King was there. We see it when President Reagan felt the anger well up within his heart at injustice that day in West Berlin and made him cry out against his aide's admonition that he take this line out of his speech: "General Secretary Gorbachev, if you seek peace, if you seek prosperity for the Soviet Union and Eastern Europe, if you seek liberalization: Come here to this gate! Mr.

Gorbachev, open this gate! Mr. Gorbachev, tear down this wall!"

When you follow these simple steps, you will develop the kind of attitude toward yourself and your ideas and your audience that will make you persuasive. Your words will carry conviction. Your delivery will be direct. Your speech will be filled with variety, vitality, and intensity, and a poise that comes through dedicating yourself to the truth of your message.

Practice Makes Perfect

A lot of your success in concentrating on the message you want to communicate and increasing the effectiveness of your delivery can be developed through rehearsal. Never forget, practice makes perfect. Everyone who wants to acquire the art of speaking must practice it.

Charles Fox was an outstanding orator in the British Parliament who supported the American Revolution and the emancipation of the slave trade. No one in England could match his skill. People had such a respect for him that they hung his picture on the wall of their homes. The King of England had his picture taken next to a bust of Charles Fox.

Charles J. Fox - 1749-1806

Fox was a man of great intellect, but this does not make someone a great orator. Fox's closest friend, Lord Erskine, attributed the secret of Fox's genius and his oratorical persuasion to his heart that was aflame with the ideals of liberty. "A cold hearted man might write a book, but it is doubtful such a person will have much effect in public discourse." He writes, "It is the heart which is the spring and fountain of eloquence ... Fox was trembling alive to every kind of private wrong or suffering and from the habitual and fervent contemplation of the just principles of government. Fox had the most bitter and inextinguishable contempt for the low arts of political intrigue, and an indignant abhorrence of every species of tyranny, oppression and injustice."[75]

Erskine tells us that Fox never concentrated on the music or intonation of his words, but always on the content. His words were colored and toned by the content. Describing the effect of his oratory, Erskine writes that Fox's sentences rapidly succeeded each other and mixed together "as lava rises in bursts from the mouth of a volcano, when the resistless energies of the subterranean world are at their height." [76]

About Fox's skill, Spurgeon writes, "It was by slow degrees that Fox became perhaps the most brilliant and powerful debater that ever lived. He attributed his success to the resolution which he formed when very young, of speaking well or ill - at least every night." Fox also made it his policy to practice speaking every night while he attended school. He stated, "During five whole sessions, I spoke every night but one, and I regret only that I did not speak on that night, too."[77]

Practice makes perfect! Spurgeon suggested to his students to practice speaking every day in their rooms, even if it was just to their own chair and books. He also suggested that practicing in public with a friend will help overcome intimidation caused by the sight of an audience. "Find a friend and practice speaking to them. Each person should take a turn at being the audience and offering each other a little friendly criticism and encouragement. Get together with a few friends, put a few topics in a bowl and draw them out at random and ask someone to speak on the topic, extemporaneously."

Never forget that conversation can be edifying as well. Remember that thought is to be linked with speech. Henry Ward Beecher - a Christian Congregationalist minister, social reformer, abolitionist, and great orator of the nineteenth-century - emphasized that we must act, speak, or write our thoughts in order for them to expand and grow. "Expression gives them development." So don't hesitate to think out loud. A great way to grow in your ability to communicate extemporaneously is to sit down and simply talk with a friend and discuss topics of interest.

When a new thought or image comes into your mind, follow that thought or that image as far as it will take you and see how it unfolds. This type of practice will be of great help when you are speaking and a new thought or image presents itself. You will have more confidence to follow it and unfold it in public, from having done this beforehand many times in private. You will eventually find that as you express the ideas you have, new ideas will follow that you haven't thought of before.

It is also very helpful to be able in your private devotion to pray with your own voice. Spurgeon explained to his students that he also found reading aloud to be more beneficial than the silent process. He found that when he was mentally working out a sermon, it was a relief to speak to himself as the thoughts flowed forth.

"Good impromptu speech," Spurgeon said, "is just the utterance of a practiced thinker - a person of information, meditating on his legs and allowing his thought to march through his mouth into the air." [78]

Never forget that the man or woman who says, "I would do great things if only I had the time," would do nothing if he or she had all the spare time in the world. There is always spare time at the disposal of every person who is willing to put forth the energy to use it. If you feel that you don't have the energy, go ahead and act anyway, just begin. Ask the Lord for His resurrection power; ask Him to increase your capacity and empower you by His Holy Spirit. "Even youths grow tired and weary, and young men stumble and fall; but those who hope in the Lord will renew their strength. They will soar on wings like eagles; they will run and not grow weary, they will walk and not be faint." (Isa. 40:30-31) Remember, you are not a "couch potato" and so you watch television. The opposite is true, because you watch too much television, you have become a couch potato - your energy has been sapped and you have been lulled to sleep.

"The Spirit who dwells in you," Paul explained, "will quicken your mortal body." (Romans 8:11) This is the promise of the New Covenant, "We have this treasure in earthen vessels that the power may be of God and not of ourselves." (2 Cor. 4:7) Soon the Power of God's Spirit will energize you, your interest will push you forward, and zeal will overcome every tiredness. But how many Christians forfeit God's great blessing by not asking for it or expecting it, and instead, wallow in the mire of self's insufficiency.

Henry W. Longfellow, nineteenth-century poet, gives us food for thought. Here is an excerpt from his *Ladder of Saint Augustine*:

> The distant mountains that uprear
> Their frowning foreheads to the skies,
> Are crossed by pathways that appear
> As we to higher levels rise.
>
> Heights by great men gained and kept
> Were not attained by sudden flight;
> But they while their companions slept,
> Were toiling upward in the night.

Standing on what too long we bore
With shoulders bent and downcast eyes,
We may discern - unseen before-
A path to higher destinies.

Nor deem the irrevocable Past,
As wholly wasted - wholly vain -
If rising on its wrecks at last
To something nobler we attain.

Ten

The Anointing Breaks the Yoke

If you are among those who want to bring messages from God or bring His wisdom to bear on life, there is one ingredient in public speaking that is essential and for which there is no substitute - the anointing of the Holy Spirit. The Bible teaches us, "Holy men of old spoke as they were moved on by the Holy Spirit." All of our rhetoric is useless unless it is inspired by God and anointed by the Holy Spirit. Regardless of our calling or field of endeavor, God can anoint us to speak on many themes for the benefit of others.

About Jesus, the people said, "Never did a man speak the way this Man speaks ... The multitudes were amazed at His teaching for He was teaching them as one who has authority, and not as their scribes." (John 7:46; Matt. 7:29)

When Jesus was arrested, the disciples cowered in fear. Peter denied he ever knew Jesus. After His resurrection, Jesus promised the disciples that He would send them "power from on high" so they have the ability to preach the gospel. On the day of Pentecost when the Holy Spirit was poured out and the one hundred and twenty disciples were baptized in the Holy Spirit, everything changed. The Bible tells us that "tongues of fire" appeared over the heads of those disciples. They went out and began speaking about Jesus and the Word of God with great boldness and authority. Their tongues and their words were on fire. Peter preached under the anointing of the Holy Spirit and three thousand people were saved in one day.

One thing is certain when you are anointed by the Holy Spirit - it is impossible for your audience to remain neutral. Stephen was a man anointed by the Holy Spirit. Stephen's preaching about Jesus' death and resurrection caused such conviction among the Jews that they stoned him to death. The Bible records, "They were unable to cope with the wisdom and the Spirit with which Stephen was speaking ... those who heard him were cut to the quick, and they began gnashing their teeth at him, they cried out with a loud voice and covered their ears and they rushed upon him with one impulse." As Stephen was speaking, they stoned him to death. (Acts 6:10,7:54,57)

Stephen's words and example were not lost on a rebellious group of people. Presiding over the stoning of Stephen that day was a young man named Saul, a great persecutor of the church who was making it his one ambition to destroy the church of Jesus Christ. Later, Saul met the resurrected Christ in a blinding light on the road to Damascus. His name was changed to Paul and he became one of the greatest apostles of Jesus Christ of all time. It is certain the testimony of Stephen continued to be a constant reminder to Paul of what it means to make a bold and fearless presentation of the Truth.

Paul's fearless messages brought both life and caused consternation. Once Paul was speaking to a group of Jews who became so angry they were trying to kill him. He was rescued and arrested by Roman soldiers for disturbing the peace. When the arresting officer learned Paul was a Roman citizen by birth, he treated him with great respect. As a Roman citizen, Paul appealed to Caesar to have his case heard. He was determined to testify to Caesar about the Living Christ. Learning of a plot against Paul's life, the Roman soldiers escorted him out of town at night surrounding him with "two hundred foot soldiers, two hundred spearmen, and seventy troops mounted on horseback." (Acts 22) This is an example of how God watches over those He has anointed to deliver a message to make certain they have the opportunity to say what He wants said.

Moving the Hearts of Your Listeners

The message you bring should have an effect on people. If people simply remain neutral after listening to you speak, it is doubtful that what you said was worth listening to. Even though the early church had been baptized in the Holy Spirit to empower them to preach the Gospel, they continually prayed for even greater boldness. Here is one of their prayers:

> Now Lord, look on their threats, and grant to Your servants that with all boldness they may speak Your word, by stretching out Your hand to heal, and that signs and wonders may be done through the name of Your holy Servant Jesus. (Acts 4:29)

The Scripture tells us their prayer was answered: "When they had prayed, the place where they were assembled together was shaken; and they were all filled with the Holy Spirit, and they spoke the Word of God with boldness." (Acts 4:29-31)

After this, Peter and John and the apostles were preaching all over Jerusalem saying that Jesus was the Jewish Messiah. The religious leaders became jealous of the apostles because so many people were turning to Jesus. The Pharisees had the apostles arrested in the temple where they were speaking and threw them in jail. At night an angel came and opened the jail and let them out. The angel told them, "Go, stand in the temple and speak to the people all the words of this life."

So as soon as the sun was up the next morning, they went back to the temple where they had been arrested and forbidden to speak and started preaching at the same spot. What boldness! When the religious leaders heard they had mysteriously escaped from jail and were back in the temple preaching again, they were furious and brought them up for questioning, demanding them to explain their disobedience. The apostles replied, "Whether it is right in the sight of God to obey you rather than God, you be the judge; for we cannot stop speaking of what we have seen and heard." (Acts 4:19-20)

Later Peter would explain to the church, "Those who preach the Gospel among you did it by the power of the Holy Spirit sent from heaven." (1 Peter 1:12) These early Christian men and women were on fire with a message from God that had changed their lives. They believed the Truth they spoke to others would change the world. And it did! Let all those who are called by His Name go and do likewise. Pray for supernatural boldness. Ask Jesus to baptize you with the Holy Spirit and fire.

And here is the good news - if you struggle with fear, you don't have to work hard to try to overcome it. Simply pray and ask God to deliver you from fear that would hold you back from speaking to others. Paul reminds us, "God has not given us a spirit of fear and timidity, but of power, of love, and of a sound mind." David gives us this word of assurance, "I sought the Lord and He answered me, and He delivered me from all my fears." (Tim.1:7; Ps.34:4) If you have prayed and asked God to deliver you from fear and you are still afraid, keep praying and asking until you experience God's full deliverance. It's worth it!

Why We Can Speak with Great Confidence

In the language of allegory, the Scriptures describe the effects of God's Word, whether spoken through us to others, by others to us, or to our heart as we meditate in His Word or as we walk along the way. The Scriptures use *lightning* as an allegorical image to represent the conviction and revelation that God's words bring.

Let's look at a few Scriptures to gain a better understanding of this metaphor. David tells us, "The Voice of the Lord is powerful," it is "majestic," it "shakes the cedars of Lebanon," it makes the "deer to calf ... the Voice of the Lord strikes with *lightning* bolts." Job tells us:

> He spreads *lightning* around Him, by these He judges the people. He covers His hands with *lightning* and commands it to strike the mark. Its noise declares His Presence. He thunders His Voice. Rumblings go out from His mouth and His *lightning* to the ends of the earth. After it, a Voice roars. He thunders with His majestic Voice. He does not restrain the *lightnings* when His Voice is heard. He disperses the cloud of His *lightning* that it may do whatever He commands it on the face of the inhabited earth. Whether for correction or for His world or for His loving kindness, He causes it to happen. [79]

The Psalmist declares, "His *lightning* lit up the world, the

earth saw and trembled, the mountains melted at the Presence of the Lord. The heavens declare His righteousness. All the peoples have seen His glory." [80] This wonderful allegory shows us the power of God's Word being spoken and preached. The Jewish sages called it, "The *lightning* flashes of new insight in Torah." [81] It shakes people from their complacency, it judges our hearts, it declares God's Presence. The anointed Word does whatever God wants it to do. It melts hard hearts, it brings joy and love, comfort and kindness. This is the value of speaking a message from God - it will find its mark and have its effect.

Hebrews says it this way, "For the Word of God is alive and powerful. It is shaper than the sharpest two edged sword, cutting between soul and spirit, between joint and marrow. It exposes our innermost thoughts and desires." (Heb. 4:12)

The Power of Preaching the Word

Luke tells us that Jesus appointed seventy-two disciples and sent them out to preach two by two to every city where He himself was to go. These were His instructions to them:

> "The harvest is great, but the workers are few. So pray to the Lord who is in charge of the harvest; ask Him to send more workers into his fields. Now go, and remember that I am sending you out as lambs among wolves" ...Then He said to the disciples, 'Anyone who accepts your message is also accepting Me. And anyone who rejects you is rejecting Me. And anyone who rejects Me is rejecting God, who sent Me."

The seventy-two came back rejoicing at the power that was in the name of Jesus and the success of their preaching mission:

> When the seventy-two disciples returned, they joyfully reported to Him, "Lord, even the demons obey us when we use Your Name!" "Yes," He told them, "I saw Satan fall from heaven like *lightning*! Look, I have given you authority over all the power of the enemy, and you can walk among snakes and scorpions and crush them. Nothing will injure you."...At that same time, Jesus was filled with the joy of the Holy Spirit, and He said, "O Father, Lord of heaven and

earth, thank you for hiding these things from those who think themselves wise and clever, and for revealing them to the childlike - to the babes. Yes, Father, it pleased you to do it this way." (Luke 10:1-19 LNT, NKJ)

Jesus rejoiced in the simple childlike faith they had as they obeyed His directions and got results. Jesus called them the "babes." He also said that they were "lambs among wolves," yet He didn't hesitate to send them out to preach His messages. He did not think that they needed to go to seminary for years to become wise before they would be qualified to preach or speak in His name. He didn't believe they were too young and inexperienced to be entrusted with the Good News.

After all, it was not the messengers that Jesus was counting on to persuade people about the Truth. He was counting on the message of Truth itself to do the work and the power of the "Holy Spirit to convict the world of sin, of righteousness and of judgment." As a result of the anointed Word being preached from these "sent out" ones, Jesus said that He saw "Satan" being cast out of the heavens, "falling like *lightning*" - displaced by the Truth that makes free! Paul reminds us that our faith must not rest on the wisdom of man to persuade, but on the power of God and the seed of Truth that we sow. The Word has the power to reveal itself and do its work long after we have finished talking.

Remember, the size of your audience and whether you are standing on a stage delivering your message is of little significance. Preaching can take place in a one on one situation or in small groups, as well as in large audiences. Don't under estimate the importance of small or seemingly insignificant things.

John Wesley was the founder of Methodism. What is known as the First Great Spiritual Awakening that swept England and Colonial America prior to the Revolutionary War started through the preaching of Wesley in England and Whitefield in America. As an Anglican minister of the Church of England, Wesley had come to America to convert the Indians. During a storm at sea, Wesley noticed that everyone on the ship was crying out in fear, except for a group of Moravians who had a deep peace in Jesus in the midst of that storm. Wesley wrote later that these Moravians had a faith that he knew he did not have. He had no assurance of his own salvation. When Wesley returned to England, he sought out the Moravians to find this faith and had an encounter with the Living Christ. From this life-altering experience at the age of 40, Wesley went everywhere calling people to "holiness of heart and life," and preaching, "You must be born-again."

Wesley was not well-received in the Church of England and they refused to let him preach in the churches. Hoping to share this new found faith with the Anglican congregations, He went back to his home parish in Epworth, England, where he grew up and where his father Samuel had been a minister for

John Wesley Preaching at Epworth on His Father's Tombstone

many years. Here was a place he felt would give him a warm reception. To his great disappointment the deacons met and refused to let him preach at Epworth because they thought he was a religious fanatic. Wesley said, "If you won't let me preach in the parish, then the world is my parish!" Wesley went outside the church building, climbed up on his father's tombstone, and preached from there. So many people came to hear him preach, Epworth parish church could have never held them anyway.

Wesley wrote the following in his journal about his determination to preach the Gospel:

Sunday a.m. May 5: Preached at St. Ann's - was asked not to come back any more.

Sunday p.m. May 5: Preached at St. John's - deacons said, "Get out and stay out!"

Sunday a.m. May 12: Preached at St. Jude's - can't go back there either.

Sunday p.m. May 12: Preached at St. George's - kicked out again.

Sunday a.m. May 19: Preached at St. Somebody Else's - deacons called a special meeting and said not to return.

Sunday p.m. May 19: Preached on the street - kicked off the street.

Sunday a.m. May 26: Preached out in a meadow - chased out of meadow when a bull was let loose during the service.

Sunday a.m. June 2: Preached at the edge of town; kicked off the highway.

Sunday p.m. June 2: Preached in pasture - 10,000 people came!

Then Wesley penned this:

Praise the Lord!
"We are fools for Christ's sake." (1 Cor. 4:10)

"But thanks be to God, who gives us the victory through   our
Lord Jesus Christ. Therefore, my beloved brothers, be steadfast,

Wesley Preaching at Charing Cross Road - *London*

immovable, always abounding in the work of the Lord, knowing that in the Lord your labor is not in vain." (1 Cor. 15:57-58)

The Spiritual Awakening that Wesley started with his tenacity to preach "holiness" and the necessity of being "born-again," anywhere and everywhere, and the large number of people Wesley raised up and commissioned to go out and preach in both England and the British Colonies (soon to become the United States of America) literally transformed the English speaking world - spiritually, morally, politically, and culturally.

His preaching directly and indirectly led to the establishment of the priesthood of the believers in such a dynamic way that this led to the overthrow of the idea of the divine right of kings and the establishment of self-government, the overthrow of slavery, the establishment of philanthropic organizations - unheard of before Wesley - education for the masses, hospitals, and much more. Because of John Wesley's boldness to preach the uncompromised Truth, the world has never been the same!

Those who have changed the world, have had this determination. Alexander the Great, head of the ancient Grecian Empire, demonstrated this:

> "Sir," the captain told Alexander, "there is a formidable army of hundreds of thousands of Persians prepared to defeat you."

> Alexander answered, "Yet, one butcher fears not thousands of sheep."

> "Ah!" said another, "When the Persians draw their bows, their arrows are so numerous that they darken the sun."

> Alexander responded, "It will be fine to fight in the shade!"

The Scriptures tell us about the tenacity of those whom God has called to speak for Him: "On your walls, O Jerusalem, I have placed watchmen. All day and all night they will never keep silent." (Isa. 62:6) Our heart cries out, "Jesus raise up men and women like this to preach the Gospel of Your kingdom!"

Remember, faith and determination makes things possible; it does not make them easy. John Milton, seventeenth-century Puritan poet and statesman, one of the most pre-eminent authors in the English language, and one of the world's great thinkers, wrote this about the power of Truth:

> Let every false doctrine loose and then bring out Truth on the field, and Truth has the power to win the day!

As we stand in the blaze of Truth, the Holy Spirit will speak to the hearts of the hearers and will do His work to "convict the world of sin, of righteousness, and of judgment" far beyond our own power to add or detract.

In the Book of Revelation, we find one of the greatest prophetic images of the power of Truth to prevail perhaps ever written. The heavenly messenger told John, "The testimony of Jesus is the spirit of prophecy." After this heaven opened, and this is what John saw:

> Then I saw heaven opened, and a white horse was standing there. Its rider was named Faithful and True, for He judges fairly and wages a righteous war. His eyes were like flames of fire, and on His head were many crowns. A name was written on Him that no one understood except Himself. He wore a robe dipped in blood, and His name was called the Word of God.
>
> The armies of heaven, dressed in the finest of pure white linen, followed Him on white horses. From His mouth came a sharp sword to strike down the nations. He will rule them with an iron rod. He will release the fierce wrath of God, the

Almighty, like juice flowing from a winepress. On His robe and on His thigh was written this title: *King of all kings and Lord of all lords* ! (Rev. 19:11-16)

And what does this tell us? Wherever God's message of Truth is proclaimed, the armies of heaven follow that Word and cause it to do the thing that God sends it to do. The "arrows" of Truth "are sharp in the hearts of the King's enemies."(Ps. 45:5) His Word will prevail and conquer. This fact is confirmed throughout the pages of Scripture. You can be confident that God's Word continues to speak after your speech is finished. Proclaim God's Word, deliver His message, and it is accompanied by the Holy Spirit's conviction and the powerful armies of heaven. "I watch over My Word to perform it," said God through the prophet. "My Word will not return void, but it will accomplish the thing that I send it to do." (Jer. 1:12; Isa. 55:11) "Heaven and earth shall pass away," Jesus declared, "but My word will never pass away."(Luke 21:33)

   In 1841, one of the great preachers of New England reflected on the power of God's Word. I will end this chapter with a lengthy quote from "What is Transient and Permanent in Christianity" by Theodore Parker because perhaps no one has ever explained the "power of Truth to win the day" better:

> Christ says, His Word shall never pass away. Yet at first sight nothing seems more fleeting than a word ... It leaves no track where it went through the air. Yet to this, and this only did Jesus entrust the Truth when He came to the earth - Truth for the salvation of the world. He took no pains to perpetuate His thoughts; they were poured forth where occasion found Him an audience - by the side of the lake, or a well; in a cottage, or the temple; in a fisher's boat, or the synagogue of the Jews.

He founds no institution as a monument to His words. He appoints no order of men to preserve His bright and glad revelations. He only bids His friends give freely the Truth they had freely received. He did not even write His words in a book. With a noble confidence, the result of His abiding faith, He scattered His words abroad on the world, leaving the seed to its own vitality.

He knew, that which is of God cannot fail, for God keeps his own. He sowed His seed in the heart, and left it there, to be watered and warmed by the dew and the rain which heaven sends. He felt His words were for eternity. So He trusted them to the uncertain air; and for thousands of years that faithful element has held them good, distinct as when first warm from His lips.

Now they are translated into every human speech, and murmured in all earth's thousand tongues...Those words have become the breath of the good, the hope of the wise, the joy of the pious, and that for many millions of hearts. They are the prayers of our churches; our better devotions by fireside and field-side; the enchantment of our hearts.

It is these words, that still work wonders, to which the first recorded miracles were nothing in grandeur and utility. It is these which build our temples and beautify our homes. They raise our thoughts of sublimity; they purify our ideal of purity: they hallow our prayer for truth and love. They make beauteous and divine the life which plain men lead. They give wings to our aspirations.

Sorrow is lulled at their bidding. They take the sting out of disease, and rob adversity of his power to disappoint. They give health and wings to the pious soul, to the broken-hearted and shipwrecked in his voyage of life, and encourage him to attempt the perilous way once more. They make all things ours: Christ our brother; Time our servant; Death our ally and the witness of our triumph.

They reveal to us the Presence of God, which else we might not have seen so clearly in the first wind-flower of spring; in the falling of a sparrow; in the distress of a nation; in the sorrow or the rapture of the world. Silence the voice of Christianity, and then far gone is that sweet music which kept in awe the rulers and the people, which cheers the poor widow in her lonely toil and comes like light through the windows of morning, to men who sit stooping and feeble, with failing eyes and a hungering heart.

Such is the life of these Words; such the empire they have won for themselves over men's minds since they were spoken first. In the meantime, the words of great men and mighty, whose name shook whole continents, though graven in metal and stone, though stamped in institutions and defended by whole tribes of priest and troops of followers - their words have gone to the ground, and the world gives back no echo of their voice.

Meanwhile the great works also of old times, castle and tower and town, their cities and their empires, have perished and left scarce a mark on the bosom of the earth to show they once have been. The philosophy of the wise, the art of the accomplished, the song of the poet, the ritual of the priest, though honored as divine in their day, have gone down, a prey to oblivion. Silence has closed over them; only their specters now haunt the earth. A deluge of blood has swept over the nations; a night of darkness, more deep than the fabled darkness of Egypt, has lowered down upon that flood, to destroy or to hide what the deluge had spared.

But through all this, the Words of Christianity have come down to us from the lips of that Hebrew youth, gentle and beautiful as the light of a star, not spent by their journey through time and through space. They have built up a new civilization, which the wisest Gentile never hoped for; which the most pious Hebrew never foretold. Through centuries of wasting, these Words have flown on like a dove in the storm, and now wait to descend on hearts pure and earnest, as the Father's Spirit, we are told, came on His lowly Son.

The old heavens and the old earth are indeed passed away, but the Word stands. Fleeting is what man calls great; how lasting what God pronounces true...The Bible has made a greater, deeper mark on the world than the rich and beautiful literature of all the heathen... But if error prevail for a time and grow old in the world, Truth will triumph at the last, and then we shall see the Son of God as He is. Lifted up, He shall draw all nations unto Him. Then will men understand the Word of Jesus, which shall not pass away. Then shall we see and love the Divine life that He lived.

How vast has His influence been. How His spirit wrought in the hearts of His disciples, rude, selfish, bigoted, as at first they were. How it has wrought in the world. His Words judge the nations. The wisest son of man has not measured their height. They speak to what is deepest in profound men; what is holiest in good men; what is divinest in religious men. They kindle anew the flame of devotion in hearts long cold.

They are Spirit and Life. His Truth was not derived from Moses and Solomon; but the light of God shone through Him, not colored, not bent aside. His life is the perpetual rebuke of all time since. It condemns ancient civilization; it condemns modern civilization. Wise men we have since had, and good men; but this Galilean youth strode before the world whole ... So much of Divinity was in Him. His Words solve the questions of the present age.

In Him the Godlike and the Human met and embraced, and a Divine Life was born. Measure Him by the world's greatest sons; how poor they are. Try Him by the best of men; how little and low they appear. Exalt Him as much as we may, we shall yet, perhaps, come short of the mark.

But still was He not our brother; the Son of Man, as we are; the Son of God, like ourselves? His excellence, was it not human excellence? His wisdom, love, piety - sweet and celestial as they were - are they not what we also may attain? In Him, as in a mirror, we may see the image of God, and go on from glory to glory, till we are changed into the same image, led by the Spirit which enlightens the humble.

Viewed in this way, how beautiful is the life of Jesus. Heaven has come down to earth, or rather, earth has become heaven. The Son of God, come of age, has taken possession of His birthright. The brightest revelation is this - of what is possible for all men, if not now, at least hereafter. How pure is His Spirit, and how encouraging its Words. "Lowly sufferer," He seems to say, "see how I bore the cross. Patient laborer, be strong; see how I toiled for the unthankful and the merciless. Mistaken sinner, see of what thou art capable. Rise up, and be blessed."

Christianity is a simple thing; very simple. It is absolute, pure Morality; absolute, pure Religion; the love of man; the love of God acting without let or hindrance. The only creed it lays down is the great Truth which springs up spontaneous in the holy heart - there is a God. Its watchword is, "Be perfect as your Father in Heaven." The only form it demands is a divine life; doing the best thing, in the best way, from the highest motives; perfect obedience to the great law of God. Its sanction is the Voice of God in your heart; the perpetual Presence of Him who made us and the stars over our head; Christ and the Father abiding within us. All this is very simple; a little child can understand it; very beautiful, the loftiest mind can find nothing so lovely.

The end of Christianity seems to be to make all men one with God as Christ was one with Him; to bring them to such a state of obedience and goodness, that we shall think Divine thoughts and feel Divine sentiments, and so keep the law of God by living a life of truth and love. Its means are Purity and Prayer; getting strength from God and using it for our fellow men as well as ourselves. It allows perfect freedom. It does not demand all to think alike, but to think uprightly, and get as near as possible to the Truth; not all to live alike, but to live holy, and get as near as possible to a life perfectly divine. Christianity gives us the largest liberty of the sons of God, and were all men Christians after the fashion of Jesus, this variety would be a thousand times greater than now; for Christianity is not a system of doctrines, but rather a method of attaining oneness with God.

It demands, therefore, a good life of piety within, of purity without, and gives the promise that who does God's will, shall know of God's doctrine.

In an age of corruption, as all ages are, Jesus stood and looked up to God. As the result of this virgin purity of soul and perfect obedience, the light of God shone down into the very depths of his soul, bringing all of the Godhead which flesh can receive. He would have us do the same; worship with nothing between us and God; act, think feel, live, in perfect obedience to Him; and we never are Christians as he was the Christ, until we worship, as Jesus did, with no mediator, with nothing between us and the Father of all.

He felt that God's word was in Him; that He was one with God. He told what He saw - the Truth; He lived what He felt - a life of Love. He brought the Truth, then His words and example passed into the world and can no more perish than the stars be wiped out of the sky. The Truths He taught; His doctrines respecting man and God; the relation between man and man, and man and God, with the duties that grow out of that relation, are always the same, and can never change till man ceases to be man, and creation vanishes into nothing.

No; forms and opinions change and perish; but the Word of God cannot fail. The Christianity holy people feel in the heart - the Christ that is born within us, is always the same thing to each soul that feels it. This differs only in degree and not in kind. This is that common Christianity, which burns in the hearts of the pious. It makes us outgrow any form, or any system of doctrines we have devised, and approach still closer to the Truth. It would lead us to take what help we can find.

Real Christianity gives us new life. It is the growth and perfect action of the Holy Spirit that God puts into the sons of men. It would make us revere the holy words spoken by "godly men of old," but revere still more the word of God spoken through Conscience, Reason, and Faith, as the holiest of all.

It would point to Him as our brother, who went before, like the Good Shepherd, to charm us with the music of His Words, and with the beauty of His life, to lead us up the steeps of mortal toil, within the gate of Heaven. It would have us make the kingdom of God on earth, and enter more fittingly the kingdom on high. It would lead us to form Christ in the heart, on which Paul laid such stress, and work out our salvation by this.

If you take the true Word of God, and live out this, nothing shall harm you. Men may mock, but their mouthfuls of wind shall be blown back upon their own face. If the Master of the house were called Beelzebub, it matters little what name is given to the household. The name Christian, given in mockery, will last till the world go down.

He that loves God and man, and lives in accordance with that love, needs not fear what man can do to him. His Religion comes to him in his hour of sadness, it lays its hand on him when he has fallen among thieves, and raises him up, heals, and comforts him. If he is crucified, he shall rise again.[82]

An Excerpt

This Present Crisis

James Russell Lowell (1819-1891)

Once to every man and nation
　Comes the moment to decide,
In the strife of Truth with Falsehood,
　For the good or evil side;
　Some great cause, God's new Messiah,
　Offering each the bloom or blight,
Parts the goats upon the left hand, and
　The sheep upon the right,
And the choice goes by forever
　'Twixt that darkness and that light.

Hast thou chosen, O my people,
　On whose party thou shalt stand,
Ere the Doom from its worn sandals
　Shakes the dust against our land?
Though the cause of Evil prosper, yet
　'Tis Truth alone is strong,
And, albeit she wander outcast now,
　I see around her throng
Troops of beautiful, tall angels,
　To enshield her from all wrong.

Backward look across the ages
　And the beacon-moments see,
That, like peaks of some sunk continent,
　Jut through Oblivion's sea;

Not an ear in court or market
  For the low foreboding cry
Of those Crises, God's stern winnowers,
   From whose feet earth's chaff must fly;
Never shows the choice momentous
  Till the judgment hath passed by.

Careless seems the great Avenger;
  History's pages but record
One death-grapple in the darkness
  'Twixt old systems and the Word;
Truth forever on the scaffold,
  Wrong forever on the throne,
Yet that scaffold sways the future,
  And, behind the dim unknown,
Standeth God within the shadow,
  Keeping watch above his own.

Then to side with Truth is noble
  When we share her wretched crust,
Ere her cause bring fame and profit,
  And 'tis prosperous to be just;
Then it is the brave man chooses,
  While the coward stands aside,
Doubting in his abject spirit,
  Till his Lord is crucified,
And the multitude make virtue
  Of the faith they had denied.

Count me o'er earth's chosen heroes,
  They were souls that stood alone,
While the men they agonized for
  Hurled the contumelious stone,

Stood serene, and down the future
  Saw the golden beam incline
To the side of perfect justice,
  Mastered by their faith divine,
By one man's plain truth to manhood
  And to God's supreme design.

By the light of burning heretics
  Christ's bleeding feet I track,
Toiling up new Calvaries ever
  With the cross that turns not back,
And these mounts of anguish number
  How each generation learned
One new word of that grand *Credo*
  Which in prophet-hearts hath burned
Since the first man stood God-conquered
  With his face to heaven upturned.

'Tis as easy to be heroes
  As to sit the idle slaves
Of a legendary virtue
  Carved upon our fathers' graves,
Worshippers of light ancestral
  Make the present light a crime;
Was the Mayflower launched by cowards,
  Steered by men behind their time?
Turn those tracks toward Past or Future,
  That make Plymouth Rock sublime?

They were men of present valor,
  Stalwart old iconoclasts,
Unconvinced by axe or gibbet
  That all virtue was the Past's;

But we make their truth our falsehood,
  Thinking that hath made us free,
Hoarding it in moldy parchments,
  While our tender spirits flee
The rude grasp of that great Impulse
  Which drove them across the sea.

They have rights who dare maintain them;
  We are traitors to our sires,
Smothering in their holy ashes
  Freedom's new-lit altar-fires;
Shall we make their creed our jailer?
  Shall we, in our haste to slay,
From the tombs of the old prophets
  Steal the funeral lamps away
To light up the martyr-briers
  'Round the prophets of today?

New occasions teach new duties;
  Time makes ancient good uncouth;
They must upward still, and onward,
  Who would keep abreast of Truth;
Lo, before us gleam her camp-fires;
  We ourselves must Pilgrims be,
Launch our Mayflower, and steer boldly
  Through the desperate winter sea
Nor attempt the Future's portal
  With the Past's blood-rusted key.

For More Inspirational Books,

Bible Studies,

and History Books

(*Written in the 19th Century*

Before the Rewrites)

Visit

www.BibleStudyBooks.com

Bibliography

Aaron, Paul, "John Adams." *We Hold These Truths*, (Maryland: Rowman and Littlefield Publishers, in association with The Colonial Williamsburg Foundation 2008).

Abraham Lincoln Online, *Lincoln at Gettysburg* <http://showcase.netins.net/web/creative/lincoln/sites/gettysburg.htm>

Bauntain, Louis M., *The Art of Extempore Speaking* (Goggle Books)

BibleResources.org <http://bibleresources.bible.com/Bquotes.php>

Booth, Catherine,"The Iniquity of State Regulated Vice," (London:Dyer Brothers,1884),14.
<http://wcbapp1.dlib.indiana.edu/vwwp/view?docId=VAB7082>

Borden, Richard C., *Public Speaking as Listeners Like It* (Harper and Bros.: New York. 1935)

Bradford, M.E., *The Trumpet Voice of Freedom: Patrick Henry of Virginia*, (Marlborough, NH: Plymouth Rock Foundation, 1991).

Burns, Ken and Paul Barnes, *Not for Ourselves Alone: The Story of Elizabeth Cady Stanton and Susan B. Anthony.* Accessed September 30, 2004. < http://www.pbs.org/stantonanthony >

Childs, Marquis, "Triumphal March Silences Scoffers," *The Washington Post* (August 30, 1963).

Chiniquiy, Charles, *Fifty Years in the Church of Rome*, Chapter 61 <http://www.biblebelievers.com/chiniquy/>

Coffin, Charles, *The Story of Liberty* (Gainesville, Fl.: Maranatha Publications, 2011 Ed.)

CT, Christianity Today, "John Huss PreReformer Reformer" <http://www.christianitytoday.com/history/people/martyrs/john-huss.html>

Dallimore, Arnold, George Whitefield,Vol.1(Westchester, Ill.: Cornerstone Books, 1980), 230.)

Dante Alighieri, *The Divine Comedy - Purgatorio, Canto X,XI* <http://www.every poet.com/archive/poetry/dante/dante_contents.htm#purgatorio>

Dienstberger, Paul R., *The American Republic: A Nation of Christians*, Chapter 3, <http://www.prdienstberger.com/nation/TBiblio.htm>

Ellis, Thomas Talbot ,"Samuel Davies, Characteristics of His Life and Message," Fire and Ice: Puritan and Reformed Writings <http://www.puritansermons.com/banner/sdavies2.htm>

Duff, Mildred, *Catherine Booth*, <http://www.fullbooks.com/Catherine-Booth1.html>

Ellis, Thomas Talbot, "Samuel Davies: Apostle of Virginia"<http://www.puritansermons.com/banner/sdavies1.htm>

Ellis, Thomas Talbot,"Samuel Davies, Characteristics of His Life and Message," Fire and Ice: Puritan and Reformed Writings <http://www.puritansermons.com/banner/sdavies2.htm>

Fox, James, *The Speeches of Charles James Fox in the House of Commons*, Vol. 1 (London: Printed for Longman, Hurst, etc., 1815).

Franklin, Benjamin, T*he Autobiography of Benjamin Franklin* <http://etext.virginia.edu/etcbin/toccer-new2?id=Fra2Aut.sgm&images=images/modeng&data=/texts/english/modeng/parsed&tag=public&part=all>

Freedman, Max, "The Big March in Washington Described as 'Epic of Democracy,'" *Los Angeles Times* (Sep. 9, 1963).

Ginsburgh, Rabbi Yitzchak, *The Hebrew Letters*, (Israel: Linda Pinsky Publications, A Division of Gal Einai Jerusalem, 1992).

Green, Roger J., *Wesleyan Holiness Clergy*, "Catherine Booth,Model Minister," October 1996, <http://whwomenclergy.org/article72.htm>

Hansen, D, D. (2003). *The Dream: Martin Luther King, Jr., and the Speech that Inspired a Nation.* (New York, NY: Harper Collins).

Harper, Judith E., *Biography, Susan B. Anthony and Elizabeth Cady Stanton*, < http://www.pbs.org/stantonanthony/resources/index.html>

Henry, Matthew, *Matthew Henry Commentary* on 2 Corinthians 2. *Strong's Concordance Online*
<http://www.blueletterbible.org/commentaries/comm_view.cfm?AuthorID=4&contentID=1753&commInfo=5&topic=2%20Corinthians&ar=2Cr_2_2>

Henry, Patrick, Full Episode, bio.truestory <http://alturl.com/mcp86>

Jacobi, Mary P., *Common Sense Applied to Woman Suffrage* (Google books),14 <http://books.google.com>

Elizabeth Cady Stanton, Quoter's book <http://www.quotersbook.com/quote.php?show=4645>

Jefferson, Thomas, *The Writings of Thomas Jefferson*, (Published by order of Joint Committee of Congress, 1853)

Kennedy, Caroline *Profiles in Courage for Our Time*, Article (Jan. 11, 1989)

Parker, Theodore, "What is Transient and Permanent in Christianity." Googlebooks.

People's World.org, Today in History: Jan Huss Burned at the Stake 600 Years Ago" July 6, 2015,<http://www.peoplesworld.org/article/today-in-history-jan-hus-burned-at-the-stake-600-years-ago/>

Putin, Valdimir, World Economic Summit, Switzerland 2009 <
http://rt.com/politics/official-word/putin-s-speech-davos-world-
economic-forum/>

Reagan, Ronald, *An American Life*, (New York: Simon and Schuster,
1990)

Reagan, President Ronald, *Speech to Britain's Parliament*, 1982.
<http://www.historyplace.com/speeches/reagan-parliament.htm>

Reformationsa.org ,"Truth Conquers, John Huss" <http://
www.reformationsa.org/truth_conquers.htm>

Rogal, Samuel J., "Toward a Mere Civil Friendship: Benjamin
Franklin and George Whitefield." *Methodist History* 1997).

Skousen, Cleon, *The Making of America*, (The National Center for
Constitutional Studies, Washington D. C. 1985).

Spurgeon, Charles H., *Lectures to My Students* (Grand Rapids. MI.
1954).

Spurgeon, Charles H., *The Autobiography of Charles H. Spurgeon*, Vol. 2,
(Google Books).

Smith, Bradford, *Dan Webster, Union Boy*, (Indianapolis: Bobs-Merrill
Co.,1954).

Stanton, Elizabeth Cady, *Eighty Years and More, Reminiscences,
1815-1897*, 21-22,<http://www.archive.org/stream/
cu31924032654315/cu31924032654315_djvu.txt>

Thatcher, Margaret, *Margaret Thatcher, the Autobiography*, Kindle
Edition.

ThinkExsist.com <http://thinkexist.com/quotation/
the_bible_is_worth_all_the_other_books_which_have/
250958.html>

Tozer, A.W., *The Divine Conquest*, (Wheaton,Ill.: Tyndale House, 1995).

Trobisch, Walter, *Martin Luther's Quiet Time*, 1975. Table Talk, <http://www.lmsusa.org/tt-11-97.htm>

Walker, George Leon, *Some Aspects of the Religious Life of New England* (New York: Silver, Burnett, and Company, 1897).

Walter and Scott, *Thinking and Speaking*, (New York: McMillian and Co., 1966).

Webster, Daniel, United States Senate, Art and History Home, Classic Senate Speeches, <http://www.senate.gov/artandhistory/ history/common/generic/Speeches_Webster_7March.htm>

Writ, William *Sketches of the Life and Character of Patrick Henry*, (Philadelphia: Published by James Webster, 1817) View online: < http://docsouth.unc.edu/southlit/wirt/wirt.html >

Endnotes

[1] Proverbs 16:18

[2] Dante Alighieri, *The Divine Comedy - Purgatorio, Canto X,* The Proud.

[3] Ibid., *Canto XI,* Sculptures on the Pavement.

[4] A.W. Tozer, *The Divine Conquest,*(Wheaton,Ill.:Tyndale House, 1995), Intro.

[5]Charles Coffin, *The Story of Liberty* (Gainesville, Fl.: Maranatha Publications, 2011 Ed.), 62-67.

[6] "Truth Conquers, John Huss," Reformationsa.org <http:// www.reformationsa.org/truth_conquers.htm>

[7] "Today in World History: Jan Hus Burned at the Stake 600 years Ago," People's World.org, July 6, 2015 <http://www.peoplesworld.org/article/today-in-history-jan-hus-burned-at-the-stake-600-years-ago/>

[8] English Bible History, *John Huss* <http://www.greatsite.com/ timeline-english-bible-history/john-hus.html>

[9] " John Huss, PreReformer Reformer," Christianity Today <http:// www.christianitytoday.com/history/people/martyrs/john-huss.html>

[10] *Ibid.,* 233-237.

[11] *Ibid.*

[12] Walter Trobisch, *Martin Luther's Quiet Time,* 1975.

[13] William Writ, *Sketches of the Life and Character of Patrick Henry,* (Philadelphia: Published by James Webster, 1817) View online: https://goo.gl/pfBPcU

[14]Paul Aaron, "John Adams." *We Hold These Truths,* (Maryland: Rowman and Littlefield Publishers, in association with The Colonial Williamsburg Foundation 2008), 86-88.

[15] Thomas Talbot Ellis, "Samuel Davies, Characteristics of His Life and Message," Fire and Ice: Puritan and Reformed Writings <http://www.puritansermons.com/banner/sdavies2.htm>

[16] Ellis, "Samuel Davies: Apostle of Virginia"<http://www.puritansermons.com/banner/sdavies1.htm>

[17] Patrick Henry, Full Episode, bio.truestory <http://alturl.com/mcp86>

[18] Paul Aaron, "John Adams."

[19] Cleon Skousen, *The Making of America,* (The National Center for Constitutional Studies, Washington D. C. 1985), 20.

[20] M.E. Bradford, *The Trumpet Voice of Freedom: Patrick Henry of Virginia,* iii.

[21] *The Writings of Thomas Jefferson,* (Published by order of Joint Committee of Congress, 1853), 38.

[22] BibleResources.org <http://bibleresources.bible.com/Bquotes.php>

[23] ThinkExsist.com <http://thinkexist.com/quotation/the_bible_is_worth_all_the_other_books_which_have/250958.html>

[24]Arnold Dallimore, George Whitefield, Vol. 1 (Westchester, Ill.: Cornerstone Books, 1980), 230.

[25] George Leon Walker, *Some Aspects of the Religious Life of New England* (New York: Silver, Burnett, and Company, 1897), 89-92.

[26]Samuel J. Rogal, "Toward a Mere Civil Friendship: Benjamin Franklin and George Whitefield." *Methodist History* 1997) 35(4): 233–243. 0026-1238

[27] Benjamin Franklin, T*he Autobiography of Benjamin Franklin,* pp. 104–108.

[28] Thomas Talbot Ellis, "Samuel Davies, Characteristics of His Life and Message," Fire and Ice: Puritan and Reformed Writings <http://www.puritansermons.com/banner/sdavies2.htm>

[29] Paul R. Dienstberger, *The American Republic: A Nation of Christians,* Chapter 3, <http://www.prdienstberger.com/nation/TBiblio.htm>

[30] *Not for Ourselves Alone: The Story of Elizabeth Cady Stanton and Susan B. Anthony.* Ken Burns and Paul Barnes. Accessed September 30, 2004. < http://www.pbs.org/stantonanthony >

[31] Elizabeth Cady Stanton, *Eighty Years and More, Reminiscences, 1815-1897,* 21-22,<http://www.archive.org/stream/ cu31924032654315/cu31924032654315_djvu.txt>

[32] *Ibid.,* 27-37.

[33] Elizabeth Cady Stanton, *Eighty Years and More, Reminiscences, 1815-1897,* 79, 83.

[34] Elizabeth Cady Stanton, *The Women's Bible,*< http://www.sacred-texts.com/wmn/wb/wb62.htm>

[35] *Biography, Susan B. Anthony and Elizabeth Cady Stanton,* Judith E. Harper. < http://www.pbs.org/stantonanthony/resources/ index.html>

[36] Mary P. Jacobi, *Common Sense Applied to Woman Suffrage* (Google books),14 <http://books.google.com>

[37] Elizabeth Cady Stanton, Quoter's book <http:// www.quotersbook.com/quote.php?show=4645>

[38] Charles Chiniquiy, *Fifty Years in the Church of Rome,* Chapter 61 <http://www.biblebelievers.com/chiniquy/>

[39] *Ibid.*

[40] *Ibid.,* Chapter 60.

[41] *Ibid.*

[42] Hansen, D, D. (2003). *The Dream: Martin Luther King, Jr., and the Speech that Inspired a Nation.* (New York, NY: Harper Collins), 58.

[43] Marquis Childs, "Triumphal March Silences Scoffers," *The Washington Post* (August 30, 1963).

[44] Max Freedman, "The Big March in Washington Described as 'Epic of Democracy,'" *Los Angeles Times* (Sep. 9, 1963).

[45] Ronald Reagan, *An American Life*, (New York: Simon and Schuster, 1990), 681.

[46] *Ibid.*,683

[47] *Ibid.*,706-707.

[48] *Ibid.*, 713.

[49] Valdimir Putin, World Economic Summit, Switzerland 2009 < http://rt.com/politics/official-word/putin-s-speech-davos-world-economic-forum/>

[50] President Ronald Reagan, *Speech to Britain's Parliament*, 1982.

[51] Charles Coffin, Introduction to *The Sweet Land of Liberty.* (Gainesville, Fl.: Maranatha Publications, 2011 Ed.)

[52] Caroline Kennedy, *Profiles in courage for Our Time*, (Jan. 11, 1989), 70.

[53] Bradford Smith, *Dan Webster, Union Boy*, (Indianapolis: Bobs-Merrill Co.,1954).

[54] United States Senate, Art and History Home, Classic Senate Speeches, Daniel Webster, <http://www.senate.gov/artandhistory/history/common/generic/Speeches_Webster_7March.htm>

[55] Roger J. Green, *Wesleyan Holiness Clergy*, "Catherine Booth,Model Minister," October 1996, <http://whwomenclergy.org/article72.htm>

[56]Mildred Duff, *Catherine Booth*, <http://www.fullbooks.com/Catherine-Booth1.html>

[57] Catherine Booth, *The Gospel Truth, Papers on Practical Religion, Female Ministry or Woman's Right to Preach the Gospel*, Chapter 7 <http://www.gospeltruth.net/booth/cath_booth/practical_religion/cbooth_prac_rel_pap7.htm>

[58] Catherine Booth,"The Iniquity of State Regulated Vice," (London:Dyer Brothers,1884),14.
<http://webapp1.dlib.indiana.edu/vwwp/view?docId=VAB7082>

[59] Roger J. Green.

[60] Margret Thatcher, *Margaret Thatcher, The Autobiography*, Kindle Edition. p. 679.

[61] A.W. Tozer, xvi.

[62] Daniel 3:15-18.

[63] Charles H. Spurgeon, *The Autobiography of Charles H. Spurgeon*,Vol. 2, (Google Books), 239.

[64] Charles H. Spurgeon, *Lectures to My Students* (Grand Rapids. MI. 1954), 141.

[65] Spurgeon, *Lectures*, 141.

[66] Louis M. Bauntain, *The Art of Extempore Speaking* (Goggle Books), 4.

[67] A.W. Tozer, xviii.

[68] M. Bauntain, *The Art of Extempore Speaking* (New York: McDevitt-Wilson's, Inc., 1923) 23

[69]Abraham Lincoln Online, *Lincoln at Gettysburg* <http://showcase.netins.net/web/creative/lincoln/sites/gettysburg.htm>

[70] Spurgeon, *Lectures*,141.

[71] Matthew Henry, *Matthew Henry Commentary* on 2 Corinthians 2. *Strong's Concordance Online* <http://www.blueletterbible.org/commentaries/comm_view.cfm? AuthorID=4&contentID=1753&commInfo=5&topic=2%20Corinth ians&ar=2Cr_2_2>

[72] Richard C. Borden, *Public Speaking as Listeners Like It* (Harper and Bros.: New York. 1935),1-13.

[73] Spurgeon, *Lectures,* 70-77.

[74] Walter and Scott, *Thinking and Speaking,* (New York: McMillian and Co., 1966), 96.

[75] *The Speeches of Charles James Fox in the House of Commons*, Vol. 1 (London: Printed for Longman, Hurst, etc., 1815), xiii-xiv.

[76] *Ibid.* , xiv.

[77] Spurgeon, *Lectures,* 149.

[78]*Ibid.*, 152-153

[79] Job 36:30-32; 37:11-13.

[80] Psalms 29:97.

[81] Rabbi Yitzchak Ginsburgh, *The Hebrew Letters*, (Israel: Linda Pinsky Publications, A Division of Gal Einai Jerusalem, 1992), 318.

[82] Theodore Parker, "What is Transient and Permanent in Christianity." Googlebooks.

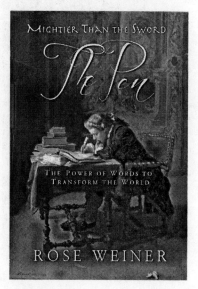

This is a course in creative writing for ages 12 through high school and adult. There are 27 chapters in this book.

Each chapter is followed by "Adventures in Writing," which include exercises to practice creative writing techniques explained and illustrated in the text.

We must write, speak or act our thoughts or they will remain in an unclear, undeveloped, and confused. Expression gives our inward feelings development.

Included in this course:

- Learn the importance of keeping a daily journal.
- Learn how to relax and to write from a place of Divine silence.
- Learn how to break writer's block and get into the flow of creativity by using clustering.
- Learn how to paint a picture with descriptive words so the reader is brought into the mood, feelings, and atmosphere of the scene.
- Learn the power of "story" from studying the writings of Harriet Beecher Stowe, Mark Twain, the poetry of John Milton, Tolkien, and others.
- Learn to write for the joy of discovery - not to just assemble facts to tell something that you know, but to write to discover what you don't know.
- Learn about the power of the written word to shape history.

Knowing how to write well and express your thoughts is extremely valuable in learning how to communicate. Becoming a great communicator is important for becoming successful in life. On a personal level being able to express your thoughts in writing will help you communicate well in your personal relationships, in the family, or in whatever circumstances you may encounter in life. This course will help you learn the skills you need to be able to write well - even if your writing is for an audience of one - it is valuable to you.

Basic Studies in Phonics, Literature, Art, Creative Writing, and History by Rose Weiner

This course focuses on the study of phonics, literature, creative writing and storytelling, drawing and painting, and the study of art and the history that it reveals. Elements of this course can be used with a wide variety of ages - from infants all the way through elementary school. Mom's will love it too!

Includes: 112 phonics/art cards and a teachers handbook.

- **Phonics -** 112 letters and letter combinations - phonetic pronunciation of the letter sounds

- **Art Appreciation -** 112 prints of beautiful paintings from Western Art of the 19th and early 20th centuries that relate to each phonogram. These paintings speak to the heart - to love of family and its values, to the love of children, of country, and of God's creation. Guided instruction on studying each painting.

- **Literature:** Over 225 selected stories with nternet links to expressive reading of free audio books. These stories are meant to furnish your child with expressive reading, good sentence structure, and good vocabulary.

- **Creative Writing and Storytelling:** Following each painting, your child is asked to write a story associated with the painting. Using the painting as a springboard to stimulate the imagination, questions are given that you can use to help your children develop their story and their own adventure.

- **Bits of Intelligence -** Bits of intelligence are presented related to the painting, - geography, cynology, ornithology, zoology, art history, history, discovery, and science - helping develop a love for learning.

- **How to Draw and Paint:** Drawing or painting exercises follow each lesson with directions and free video links featuring step by step instruction. Both you and your child will be encouraged at just how well anyone can draw when someone shows you how.

Available at weinermedia.com

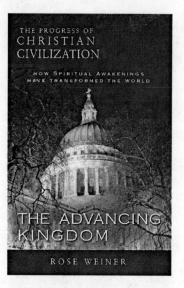

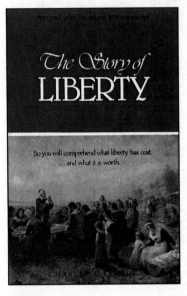

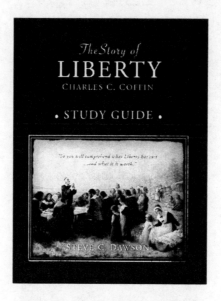

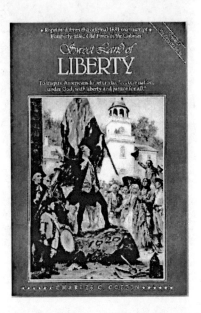

Study the Great Ideas of Christian Liberty

Sweet Land of Liberty Study

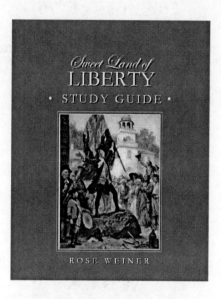

Analyze the Development of Christian
Self-Government and Religious Freedom

Rose Weiner leads students into a guided study of Coffin's *Sweet Land of Liberty.* Analyze the important events in the development of Liberty. Recognize the Hand of God's Providence moving through historical events as the colonies grow and flourish. Learn how the idea of Christian self-government and freedom of religion, assembly, and freedom of the press were hammered out from the teaching of the Bible. Learn how people raised under bigotry and intolerance broke free from these Old World concepts to embrace the principles of Liberty that are now our heritage.

The Mayflower Compact, John Locke on the Laws of Nature and Civil Government, the First Amendment and other historical documents are introduced with the text. Poetry and literature that express the ideas of our Founders are brought into the study to make this an intellectual and spiritual feast. Each chapter of this 120-page guide has fill-in-the-blanks and essay questions to help facilitate personal and group study sessions, classroom, or home schooling classes. Size 8.5 x11.

Discounts available at www.weinermedia.com

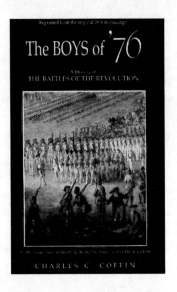

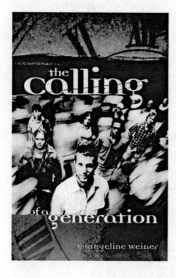

The Bible, the Cornerstone of Our Free Republic

Study the Bible

"It is impossible to govern the world without God and the Bible." *George Washington*

Establish Your Faith on the Word of God!

Are we doing a good enough job teaching the Bible to our children? Now you can make sure that you and your family have a strong foundation in God's Word.

In *The Bible Studies for a Firm Foundation* you will learn what the Bible teaches about *Repentance, Salvation, Baptism in Water, How to Grow in Your Friendship with Jesus, the Power of the Holy Spirit, Prosperity Economics and Giving, Christian Character, Worship, Prayer, Faith* and much, much more. This 232 page 8.5" x11" workbook is full of questions and answers - look them up in the Bible and let the Bible speak for itself - then fill in the blanks. This book is ideal for personal, group, homeschool, classroom, or family studies. A gold mind!

"A few years after coming to Christ we decided to go to seminary. It was intimidating, since we had only been Christians for a few years. However, we were amazed at the "firm foundation" we had from your study, and we realized we were much more prepared and had a better understanding of basic Bible principles than most of the people there!"

- David and Debbie Lowe

The Bible, the Cornerstone of Our Free Republic

Study the Bible

"The Bible is a book worth more than all the other books that were ever printed." — Patrick Henry

"The Word of God Implanted in Your Heart Has The Power to Save Your Soul!"- James 1:21

There is no other book like the book of James in the entire Bible. Written by James, Jesus very own flesh and blood brother, there is no other book so close to the heart of Jesus' teaching in the Sermon on the Mount. From his first hand experience in observing the life of Jesus, James gives us a look at what the Nature of God is really like. What is so stunning about that? This is the very same New Nature that we have inherited from Jesus Christ when we were born again which makes us sons and daughters of God!

We invite you to the banqueting table to meet Jesus in His word. Look into the "Glory" and "be transformed" into His image through the power of the Holy Spirit. In *How to Live a Life of Excellence - A Study of James,* learn:

- How to Live a Life of Faith
- How to Live in the Will of God
- How to Change Your Words and Change Your Life...and much more!
- How to Be a Doer of the Word
- How to Become God's Friend
- How to Receive the Wisdom of God
- How to Live in God's Blessing

This easy to use question answer workbook, fill in the blank format lets the Bible speak for itself. Ideal for personal, group or homeschool study. Size 8.5 x11 - 120 pages.

Discounts available at www.weinermedia.com

CPSIA information can be obtained
at www.ICGtesting.com
Printed in the USA
FFOW03n2141100518
46504473-48446FF